The InuYasha Experience

Fiction, Fantasy and Facts

cocoro books

Published by DH Publishing, Inc.
2-31-16-903 Akabane-Kita, Kita-Ku, Tokyo 115-0052, Japan
www.dhp-online.com

cocoro books is an imprint of DH Publishing, Inc.

First published 2004

Text and illustrations © 2004 by DH Publishing, Inc.

Printed in USA

Printed by Delta Printing Solutions, Inc.
Compiled by Kazuhisa Fujie and Martin Foster
Publisher: Hiroshi Yokoi
Publications Director: Clive Victor France
Design: Yoshiaki Matsusawa
Editor: Takako Aoyama
ISBN 1-932897-08-9

The InuYasha Experience

How to Use
In this book, the fifth in the popular Mysteries and Secrets Revealed! anime series, you'll find everything you need to know about InuYasha and much more! And it's so easy to use! Just follow the simple InuYasha code below and within a few hours you'll be an InuYasha expert.

Questions and Answers
Want to find out why who did what when and where? Then this is the book for you. 56 questions and detailed answers on every InuYasha topic, from characters and relationships to fighting techniques and force fields.

Glossary
When you speak the lingo everything is so much easier. At the back of this book you'll find a glossary stuffed full of names, what they mean and which pages to find them on.

Keyword Index
Want to go straight to Higurashi Shrine? Then start at the alphabetical Keyword Index at the back of the book. There you'll find page links to every destination in the InuYasha world.

InuYasha Files & Goods
Scattered throughout this book are 16 fun articles that introduce you to the more obscure side of InuYasha. Check out the meaning of "inu" and "yasha", the taste of InuYasha cookies, the story behind the name "Kagome", the Era of Warring States, and InuYasha stationery, InuYasha towels, InuYasha cell phone covers, InuYasha tea cups and InuYasha postcards!

CONTENTS

Naraku - Evil Incarnate & Super Demon

Other InuYasha Inhabitants

InuYasha Profiles

InuYasha Files

InuYasha Goods

Overview

Like many of today's popular anime, the story of InuYasha was launched in manga format. Created by Rumiko Takahashi and serialized in Shonen Sunday magazine from the autumn of 1996, InuYasha continues to be a much-loved tale in Japan.

The basic story is of the hero, InuYasha, and the heroine, Kagome, traveling through 15th and 16th century Japan - sengoku jidai, or Era of Warring States - to recover the fragments of the Shikon no Tama - literally, "the jewel of the four souls" - which will grant their every desire.

Kagome is in her final year at junior high school, and lives in the long-established Higurashi Shrine. She lives out her life like any ordinary girl, but on the very day of her 15th birthday she enters a time warp and is thrown back to the Era of Warring States through a portal in the bottom of the shrine well. There she meets InuYasha - the demi-demon.

50 years prior to this, InuYasha was sealed in a sacred tree by a spell cast by the priestess, or miko, Kikyo, after a struggle over the jewel, which InuYasha covets in order for him to become a full-fledged demon. He is set free from the spell when the jewel reemerges, and the fight for it begins all over again.

But the jewel shatters into many fine fragments, and Kagome is ordered by Kaede - the younger sister of Kikyo and also a priestess - to track down and recover each and every one of the pieces. That is how Kagome comes to set off in search of the fragments of the Shikon jewel alongside InuYasha.

Merely obtaining a single shard of the jewel leads to an exponential increase in the powers of the holder. This explains why a myriad of demons seek them as well, and why the search becomes a battle of wits and supernatural powers. Kagome and InuYasha must defeat one group of demons after another as their adventures bring them closer to the fragments of the all-important jewel.

On their travels Kagome and InuYasha come across such characters as the demon fox Shippo, the mysterious Buddhist monk Miroku and the daughter of a family of demon-exterminators, Sango. For one reason or another all these characters band together to form the toughest gang of jewel-seekers in all the warring period.

They also aim to chase up their nemesis Naraku - archrival for the scattered fragments of the Shikon jewel.

What we can immediately see is that by establishing the story as a perilous voyage of discovery and recovery during the Era of Warring States, and expanding the cast as the story progresses, InuYasha is being positioned as a long-running epic tale of derring-do.

All this time, however, we have no way of knowing what will actually happen when all the widely scattered shards of the jewel are recovered and brought together again.

Nor should we forget the unique sense of humor that is an integral part of the world of Rumiko Takahashi - nor the puppy-love that is a normal part of every 15-year-old's life. Both these elements are skillfully woven into the story to make it ever more interesting.

Many of the mysteries posed early on in the story are solved as it progresses. But it is important to remember that InuYasha is an ongoing project, and as such there are still many unsolved mysteries out there. So, stay tuned.

Rumiko Takahashi and her world

A Libra, born October 10, 1957 in Niigata, Rumiko Takahashi is blood type A, in common with many Japanese people.

She made her manga debut with Katte na Yatsura, published while she was still at Nihon Joshi Daigaku, (Japan Women's University) in 1978. Urusei Yatsura was serialized in Shonen Sunday the same year. In 1996 Takahashi was awarded the 47th Shogakukan Manga Prize for the immensely popular InuYasha, the second time for her to receive the award. Her other works include Maison Ikkoku and Ranma 1/2.

Rumiko Takahashi is unique in that she continues to draw mainly for boy's magazines. In that sense it can be said that her work is popular enough to appeal to both boys and girls.

It is also interesting to note that despite the successes of Takahashi's other work, InuYasha didn't exactly get off to a sensational start. It kind of started low-key, and for a long time showed no signs of being animated for television.

Still, it was really only a question of time, as the manga grew in popularity with each issue. Once the TV series was officially decided on, it became a major production.

Among the reasons why it took so long to come to the small screen, one important factor was the time it took for the story to hit its stride. Both the manga and the TV anime series are still running, with both popularity and viewing ratings maintaining high levels amid hopes that Takahashi may be able to carve out yet another masterpiece as she enters her

50s.

Let's take a quick look at some of Rumiko Takahashi's other works, how they were positioned relative to the period in which they were produced, and what kind of impact she and her work have had on other creators of the time.

Urusei Yatsura broke down the division between gag- and story-based manga, and is recognized today as a groundbreaking story that successfully combines jokes, science fiction and on-campus romance.

InuYasha: Love that Transcends Time (2001, Toho) Flyer (7X10 inch) $1.00

The concept played well into the medium of TV, which allowed for a host of ever more original characters to crisscross the story and the screen, pushing the limits of the manga frontier further and further into uncharted territory.

The characters and the story development owe a lot to that unique mode of expression known as "Rumiko's World," which has had both a direct and indirect impact on the works of other manga artists of the period.

Ranma 1/2 was serialized during a boom in martial arts, and the story is unique in that it combines elements not only of a hero who can freely flit between male and female identities, but also of romance in the martial arts world.

Having said that, Ranma 1/2 did not influence other works in the way that Urusei Yatsura did, mainly because it merely rode the trend of the times, breaking little new ground.

Ranma 1/2 did have at least one major achievement. It successfully coaxed girls into the world of boy's magazines, increasing overall readership. In the future, when there is no longer a barrier that separates boys and girls magazines, Ranma 1/2 is likely to be reevaluated as manga that struck a blow for equality of the sexes, putting it far ahead of its time.

InuYasha appears to start out with a set of well-used story elements - demons, time warps, role-playing, and a struggle to obtain something beyond the scope of commonly held human knowledge - the Shikon jewel.

In that sense, it is difficult to call it overridingly original. Indeed, when it was first serialized criticism was voiced about the similarity between

Urusei Yatsura: Only You (1983, Toho)
Poster (20X29 inch) $20.00

InuYasha and other manga. Some even accused Takahashi of lifting Kagome's time warp directly from Fire Tripper. Others pointed to the similarity between the confinement and release of InuYasha and parts of Ushio to Tora by Kazuhiro Fujita.

However, if we accept similarities with existing works as a done thing, we can see that by also including references to other classic tales, such as Nanso Satomi Hakkenden and Taketori Monogatari, there is a very clear possibility that Takahashi was attempting to carve out a new all-embracing form of fairy tale.

While InuYasha broadly stays within the framework of these existing works, it is not merely restricting itself to their limitations, but is instead redefining a unique worldview.

In the early days of Ranma 1/2, there was the feeling that Takahashi was keeping a careful eye on reader opinion before pushing ahead. This contributed to the impression that the story was slow to get started.

This is certainly not the case with InuYasha.
If anything, InuYasha gives the impression of a work penned with a strong sense of self-belief and a determination to get the story up and running properly.

Even while critics carped and complained about its resemblance to other works, the story ploughed ahead, forcing the reader to keep up with each new development. That is what succeeded in capturing the hearts of many readers.

Originally, my personal impression was that some of the adversaries in InuYasha, such as Mukadejoro and Shibugarasu, were under-developed and rather featureless. However, Takahashi certainly succeeds with such characters as Sakagami no Yura and Sesshomaru.

InuYasha
──Demi-Demon & Anime Star

InuYasha Profile 001
Name: InuYasha

InuYasha is a demi-demon, born of a human mother and a demon father. Both parents died while he was still young. He is estimated to be 15 years of age, and leads a lonely existence, looked down upon by the demon full-bloods because he is only half demon and incapable of living as an ordinary human being.

As a result, he develops an independent, stand-alone view on life, saying "I will get whatever it is I want based entirely on my own merits." To achieve this, he reasons that he needs to become a full-blooded demon. He sets his mind on acquiring the Shikon jewel, which will see these wishes granted.

Things change when he meets Kagome. She is the first person he can really open up to, and he suddenly realizes that he wants to protect her, and so begins a new page in the emotional and mental development of our hero.

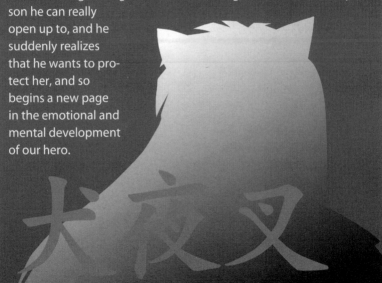

01 What's all this about demons, ghosts and spirits?

The demons are the eerie, mythological entities scattered throughout Japan. They take on many local names, but it is their ability to change appearance and pop up in the most unlikely places that makes people fear them as spirits and monsters.

In common with other superstitious peoples around the world, Japanese of old would have looked on such natural phenomena as typhoons as the embodiment of evil spirits. Illness would also have been thought of as the intrusion of an evil spirit into the body, and unhappiness in general attributed to the shenanigans of the spirit world.

It follows that these superstitions ebb and flow according to the vicissitudes of the historical and social landscape, and we can surmise that the world of InuYasha - caught up as it were in the chaos of the Era of Warring States - saw more than the usual number of natural phenomena blamed on the ill feelings of the spirits.

S ee Glossary
Demon
InuYasha
Era of Warring
 States

But what's the difference between a demon and an evil spirit, you may ask? Well, a demon is a mythological being that, because it is alive, can be killed. In a sense, there is a similarity with such legendary creatures as the Loch Ness Monster and the Abominable Snowman of the Himalayas. And that also explains how we arrive at such characters as Sango and the spirit-exterminators.

See Glossary
Sango

Other examples from Japanese myth and handed-down legend include the ugly old sand woman, Suna-kake-baba, who throws sand at travelers, blinding them, while she chuckles about it and disappears.

There is also Grandpa Crybaby, or Konakijiji, who appears before travelers as a crying child. But when he is picked up to be soothed, it immediately becomes apparent that he is in fact an old man. Once discovered, the old man becomes heavier and heavier, until he is dropped, laughing hysterically.

These characters appeared in the manga Gegegeno Kitaro, which was a hit long before the days of InuYasha, and show how close ghouls, ghosts and spirits are to the everyday lives of ordinary Japanese.

Many of the demons that appear in InuYasha are also based on Japanese myth and legend, and reworked by the author Rumiko Takahashi.

On the other hand, evil spirits are the spirits of those people who have died untimely, unhappy or unfortunate deaths and pass away with feelings of unfulfilled desire, revenge, and often with curses on their lips. Such souls are unable to enter the spirit world, and end up lingering on earth fated to make people unhappy and miserable by communicating the deep-seated grudges they hold.

In InuYasha we come across Mayu, the evil spirit of a young girl who died in a fire.

Unlike the spirit-exterminators, only a Buddhist priest who has undergone meditative discipline is capable of suppressing an evil spirit, and I guess we can say that the work of Miroku is close to this.

In a way, Sango and her spirit-exterminators are like Ghost-busters, while Miroku is closer to The Exorcist.

See Glossary
Mayu
Miroku

See questions
2 21

02 If InuYasha is a demi-demon then why does he take the side of humans?

Many of the demons are rowdy, desperado types. They are strong but chaotic, and prone to violence, turning much of their malevolence on humans. But that does not necessarily mean that all demons are evil. Some demons even do things to help human beings.

Let's put it this way: demons have their own way of thinking about and doing things. They are basically hedonistic, pleasure-seekers and don't feel they have to fall in with the human order.

InuYasha, on the other hand, is half-human, so he is able to understand the way that humans think and fit in with their way of doing things, all the while keeping the lid on his own thrill-seeking urges. Still, he may appear to lean too far in one direction when he develops feelings for Kagome, even fighting to protect her.

He has no beef with the demons that are out to help humans. He fights to gain as many fragments as possible of the Shikon jewel so he can become a full-blooded demon, and throws in his lot with Kagome and Kaede.

See Glossary
Demon
InuYasha
Shikon jewel
Kaede

See questions
1 3 4

03 What kind of demon was InuYasha's father?

The story has it that InuYasha's father was a big-shot demon in the land of the west, but he is killed in a battle with a demon called Ryukossei who possesses extraordinary powers.

In terms of appearance, InuYasha's father resembles the white lions or temple dogs of Chinese legend - more the athletic appearance of a lion than a dog.

While it is not fully explained in the story, when we realize he resembles beasts that worked in the service of the gods, and that he falls in love with a human - the mother of InuYasha - there is something that makes us think he was a good demon who was on the side of the humans.

This is also the case with the sword, Tenseiga - literally, "the fang heavenly life" or "the healing blade" - that is fashioned from a fang that he leaves to his elder son, Sesshomaru. A single swing of the sword is enough to save 100 lives. The life-giving Tenseiga is in contrast to Tessaiga - literally, "the steel-crushing fang" - that is a destructive killing blade.

See Glossary

InuYasha
Demon
Ryukossei
Sesshomaru
Tenseiga

See questions

4

InuYasha File 001

The Era of Warring States

The Era of Warring States, or sengoku jidai, was a period of cruel and hard-fought civil wars that began in 1467 with the War of Onin and came to a close around 1600, just after Hideyoshi Toyotomi succeeded in unifying Japan before his death in 1598.

It was a period in which the emperor lost all authority, and that of the Bakufu was greatly weakened, leaving Japan without any effective central power. This resulted in the emergence of sengoku daimyo - regional warlords who maneuvered and manipulated in an attempt to expand their areas of influence.

The one overriding feature of this period is chaos. This, it is believed, was the source of the many tales of demons, demigods and other delegates of evil that sprang up at that time. It is a fitting backdrop for the story of InuYasha.

In InuYasha, we see a group of people chaotically attempting to fight off the influence of demons in a world thrown off kilter by a pervading sense of evil. This mirrors the acts of betrayal and cruelty going on around them in a state where law and order no longer hold sway.

Although the warring period stretches for over 100 years, we can place the meeting of Kagome and InuYasha around 1500. This can be explained by the fact that the Shikon jewel resurfaces every 500 years. As we know that the appearance of the jewel in Kagome's left side happens around the year 2000, this places the world of InuYasha around 1500.

04 What kind of person was InuYasha's mother?

InuYasha's mother is believed to have died when InuYasha was still very young. From what we know of her, clothed in a traditional 12-layer kimono, her black hair long flowing as she rides in the back of an ox cart, she is very much the model of a Heian noblewoman.

But given that the Heian period lasted some 400 years, from the end of the 8th century to the end of the 12th century, her appearance places her in an entirely different period to the world of InuYasha and Kagome.

Although we know that InuYasha was sealed up in a sacred tree for 50 years, the arithmetic still doesn't add up. We are therefore forced to fall back on the belief that because InuYasha is half-demon, he has a lifespan that far outstrips that of humans.

Having said that, we also know that InuYasha's mother gave him a fire-resistant set of clothes - known as hinezumi no koromo, or "robe of the fire-mouse" - the red suit we see

See Glossary
InuYasha

him in all the time.

This robe actually appears in one of the classics of Japanese literature - Taketori Monogatari (Tale of the Bamboo Cutter).

The story originates around the year 900, and tells of a princess - Kaguyahime - who comes to earth from the moon. A poor bamboo cutter discovers her as a tiny baby in a bamboo stem and takes her home with him. She grows up into a beautiful princess and has many suitors, from whom she demands the hinezumi no koromo as the price of her hand in marriage.

Does this mean then that InuYasha's mother is Kaguyahime? It does seem to fit in with the Heian image of the clothing she wears. However, we know from the InuYasha movie that his mother's name is Izayoi, which appears to rule out the Kaguyahime theory.

The series is still ongoing, and when we think back to the circumstances of hinezumi no koromo, it's not too far fetched to hold out for an explanation of the connection between InuYasha's mother and Kaguyahime.

See Glossary
InuYasha
Izayoi

See questions
3

05 What are InuYasha's killer fighting techniques?

InuYasha excels in hand to hand combat, as he can literally tear his adversaries apart with his ten sharp claws. His killer technique - the Sankontesso, or "spirit-scattering claws of steel" - that is powerful enough to tear apart steel makes it easy for him to rip his demon enemies in half.

InuYasha also uses a technique known as Hijin-Kesso - "flying blade of blood" - to inflict great injury on adversaries from afar. With this technique, InuYasha splashes blood on the end of his claws and flings them boomerang-like to cleave his opponent in two.

This technique gets him out of a tight spot in a scene where InuYasha has been bound up with demon-hair by Sakasagami no Yura. Still, it's a technique that requires him to spill his own blood, so we can suppose it's not one he uses too often. Once he acquires the Tessaiga from his father, he seldom resorts to the Hijin-Kesso technique. In time, we find out that Tessaiga has extremely effective attack capabilities, but it takes us until midway through the series to realize this.

See Glossary

InuYasha
Sankontesso
Demon
Sakasagami no Yura
Tessaiga

06 Is it true that InuYasha has a heightened sense of smell?

We only have to remember that InuYasha is part dog-demon to understand why he has a powerful sense of smell - one thousand times more powerful than that of humans. This hyper-sense of smell makes it possible for him not only to pick up the scent of demons at a distance, but also to know their types and numbers.

There is a scene where the elder brother of InuYasha - Sesshomaru - is able to learn the entire goings-on in a village a long way off merely through his sense of smell. InuYasha's powers are equal to those of Sesshomaru. He figures out that Kagome is the reincarnation of Kikyo from her smell alone. The downside to this powerful sense of smell is that InuYasha is sometimes overwhelmed by strong odors if he comes into close proximity to them.

S ee Glossary
InuYasha
Demon
Sesshomaru
Kikyo

See questions
3 7

07 Does InuYasha have any weaknesses?

InuYasha is one of the strongest of the demons, and once he masters his sword - the Tessaiga - he gives the impression of being invincible. He does, in fact, have two key weaknesses.

The first is the word "Sit!"

Kaede, the younger sister of Kikyo, hangs a string of beads called kotodama nenju (word-spirit rosary beads) around InuYasha's neck. When she utters the word "Sit!" it is as though the beads become remarkably heavy, forcing InuYasha, as if by a spell, neck-first to the ground, where he lies incapable of moving.

Kotodama, or word-spirit, is an ancient belief in which words are used not only to convey meaning, but to summon up the very images of the words intoned. This is why the Japanese have a highly developed sense of the kind of words to avoid on specific occasions. For example, they will avoid any reference to division, parting or discord at marriage ceremonies, or falling, slipping or failing when refer-

S ee Glossary

InuYasha
Demon
Tessaiga
Sit
Kaede
Kikyo
Kotodama
nenju

ring to examinations.

It is Kagome who decides on the key word "Sit!" after she notices InuYasha's dog-like ears, and there is a clear master-pet relationship in the way InuYasha is unable to oppose the command. Further evidence of the master-pet relationship can be seen in the fact that this command is used less and less as InuYasha develops feelings of protectiveness for Kagome and ceases to oppose her.

InuYasha's other great weakness is the night of the new moon. On this night he suddenly loses his entire demon-like qualities and reverts to being an ordinary human teenage boy. He loses his fangs and claws, and his hair becomes increasingly black - just like any other young Japanese (or until recently, before everyone in Japan decided on a hair color anything but black!). It is not just his outward appearance that changes. All his powers, including his very vitality, fall to levels where they are no different to those of human beings.

The moon represents the Yin - the negative or dark side of the power balance, and the full moon sees not only InuYasha, but all other demons as well, morph into their most powerful state. So it follows that on the night on the new moon, when the moon has not even really begun to wax, that all his powers are nullified.

See questions
3 6

08 Why do InuYasha's eyes sometimes turn red?

rom around the middle of the series there are more and more scenes where InuYasha's eyes turn red, leading him to run amok. This happens because his thrill-seeking demon side begins to outweigh his human side as he gets older. Things are even tougher for InuYasha because his father was such a powerful demon. This means that once he awakes to the demonic qualities in his personality he turns into an uncontrollable killing machine. This alters the composition of his physical being. Once he has experienced the changes that send him into violent fits, he loses whatever it was that originally made him InuYasha, and he ends up becoming a terrifying presence fated to reap death and destruction for all his time on earth. His demonic powers are so terrible that even his own brother - Sesshomaru - fears him. It is only Tessaiga that prevents InuYasha being totally taken over by the demonic powers. While he has the sword he is safe. But once he releases it, he falls prey to his demonic side and goes out of control.

See Glossary
InuYasha
Demon
Sesshomaru
Tessaiga

See questions
1 **2**

InuYasha Banner

Banners are very much part of Japanese culture. The decorated cloth flags that can be seen flapping in almost every samurai movie battle scene still decorate Japan's cities, although today they are used mostly for advertising.

In the Era of Warring States, the period in which InuYasha is set, these rigid upright flags would have mostly depicted clans, armies and righteous words of victory.

This little brightly-colored InuYasha banner is therefore in keeping with the style of the day, although the plastic pole and rubber sucker are obviously a modern addition.

Although merely decorative, the sucker suggests that the InuYasha banner should be stuck somewhere. That would depend on the whim of the owner. However, it would probably look good on a bedroom or car window, a bathroom mirror, a computer screen, or even a fish tank.

$4.00
Size 8 cm X 26 cm
© Takahashi Rumiko/
Shogakkan/Yomiuri
TV/Sunrise 2000

InuYasha's father crafts the Tessaiga from one of his own fangs, which is then forged into a sword by the legendary sword smith, Totosai. This is the sword InuYasha's father bequeaths to InuYasha as a keepsake.

At full strength, Tessaiga encompasses an awesome power capable of killing 100 opponents with a single stroke. The fierce shock wave produced by this power is known as Kaze no Kizu - literally, Wound of the Wind.

Tessaiga looks like an old rusty sword. But once InuYasha fuses it with his powers, its very shape changes, and it becomes a sharp-edged weapon of battle.

Tessaiga is endowed with peculiar qualities that make it impossible for demons to touch it. It was originally hidden in the grave of InuYasha's father, which, for good measure, is in a pearl lodged in InuYasha's right eye.

All this is enveloped in a force field that not even Sesshomaru can enter. InuYasha can enter this force field, but is unable to unsheathe

See Glossary

Tessaiga
Totosai
InuYasha
Kaze no Kizu
Demon
Sesshomaru

his sword once there, and it is left to Kagome to do this for him. From all this it is evident that Tessaiga has no desire to be touched by those who have no interest in protecting human beings. We can surmise that InuYasha's father had the sword made with the purpose of protecting his wife once he was dead.

These are not the only strange powers Tessaiga is endowed with. The blade can also produce a force field to defend the holder against enemies. This power extends to the sheath.

Tessaiga also works to keep a lid on InuYasha's demonic urges. When InuYasha is taken over by his demon instincts, which seep through every pore of his body, his very expression turns evil and he launches into an uncontrollable rampage. It appears that his father bequeathed Tessaiga to him to stave off this very tendency.

Tessaiga is broken at one stage of the adventure. The sword smith Totosai manages to patch it back together again by splicing in one of InuYasha's own fangs. But the revamped sword is incredibly heavy, and not even InuYasha can wield it as before.

Tessaiga was originally extremely heavy, and it was only thanks to the intervention of

InuYasha's father that it became lighter. Indeed, it is his father who has protected InuYasha so far. By splicing a piece of his own fang into the sword, InuYasha has effectively taken on the task of protecting himself.

InuYasha must now go about strengthening himself in order to be able to wield this heavy sword as he did the lighter one before it. He passes the test by defeating Ryukotsusei, his father's nemesis and killer. That leaves him able to swing the sword as easily as he did before.

After vanquishing Rukotsusei, Tesseiga is permanently protected by the power of the Kaze no Kizu, and InuYasha is able to exhibit his full powers. It is also in the wake of his victory over Ryukotsusei that InuYasha is initiated into one of the deepest secrets of the Tessaiga - the Bakuryuha - which enables the sword to repel the powers of attackers and turn them against the opponent.

So what we are experiencing is a mysterious weapon that is developing and growing along with InuYasha. In this sense there are probably more secrets still to be revealed.

See Glossary
Ryukotsusei

See questions
3 **35**

If "inu" means "dog" then what is a "yasha"?

Originally taken from "Yaksa", the name of the north Indian god of fertility, the pronunciation was altered to "Yasha" to fit the readings of the Chinese characters as the belief filtered through China to Japan.

Yaksa was originally worshipped as a benevolent deity who came to be seen as a fantastic, fanged, human-devouring demon following the invasion by an entirely different tribe with different set of deities. Many modern Japanese hold this image of Yasha as an evil god, as he is generally depicted with a frightening face.

Yaksa was eventually restored to the pantheon of goodness following yet another change in religious values. However, he could never shake off the collateral baggage of being a beast-like god who succeeds in acquiring human form after a thousand years of meditative discipline and privation, finally being recognized as the penultimate deity.

It was with the dual faces of good and evil that the god Yasha arrived in Japan by way of China. It is not too difficult to suppose that Rumiko Takahashi focused on this duality of character, this internal fight between good and evil, when she set about naming her character "InuYasha".

As a result, it is no surprise to see that the half-human/demi-demon InuYasha can be both gentle as the human moment allows, or take on the appearance of the most terrifying of devils when he is unable to control his burning demon blood.

10 Kagome or Kikyo - who does InuYasha really love?

Some 50 years ago InuYasha was sealed in the sacred tree by Kikyo using hama no ya, the charmed arrows that ward off evil spirits. Therefore, Kikyo should be InuYasha's enemy. However, in the world of 50 years ago they were lovers!

Kikyo was bound by the rules of her vocation as a miko priestess to lead the life of a stoic, which meant not allowing her own emotions to become known to those around her. Because of this she was able to empathize with the demi-demon InuYasha, who led a desolate, solitary life and was understood by no one. Those feelings of empathy subsequently turned to love.

For his part, InuYasha also holds feelings of love for Kikyo, and at one stage pledges to use the Shikon jewel to become a full-fledged human being and live out his natural life with her.

But poor Kikyo falls prey to the plots and manipulations of Naraku, and seals

See Glossary

InuYasha
Kikyo
Sacred tree
Miko
Shikon jewel
Naraku

InuYasha in the sacred tree using the charmed arrow after believing herself betrayed by him. She goes to her own death holding the jewel to her breast, and it is buried along with her.

It is only after InuYasha is released that he realizes that Kikyo is dead. He then vows that he will never again let a woman that he loves die.

It is natural that he is drawn to Kagome, for she is the reincarnation of Kikyo. But Kikyo herself is brought back to life by a spell cast by an old demon witch called Urasue, and InuYasha shows signs of returning to his original love.

See Glossary
Urasue

Kagome is jealous of this, and vents her frustration on InuYasha, accusing him of two-timing her. InuYasha is in a bind, as both women are dear to him, and it is difficult for him to say he loves one more than the other...because they are really one and the same.

11 Is the flea Myogajii really InuYasha's bodyguard?

Myogajii, the flea demon, has been a retainer for the InuYasha family since InuYasha's father's time. He had great respect for the father, and now wants to pass on his deep knowledge and life experiences to InuYasha.

At just seven millimeters tall, it would be nice to think of Myoga as a tower of parasitic strength...if it were not for his annoying habit of running away when the going gets tough.

As a flea, he lives by sucking blood, and has developed a taste for that of the InuYasha family. He thrives on this blood, growing bigger the more he drinks. It is said that he can grow as tall as two meters. Along with the blood, however, he also manages to suck out poisons that threaten InuYasha's life at various stages of the story.

See Glossary
Myogajii
Demon
InuYasha

See questions

InuYasha Postcard Set

To celebrate of the release of InuYasha THE MOVIE Swords of an Honorable Ruler is this set of five InuYasha postcards.

Enclosed in an elegant double-sided vinyl pouch are five laminated postcards that depict some of the most exciting scenes from the movie.

Naraku: With sword unsheathed, he looks particularly evil in this purple and black rendition of the Evil One.

InuYasha & Friends: A thoughtful InuYasha is shown alongside Miroku and Sango, and below, in a separate frame, is Kagome about to unleash one of her magical arrows.

InuYasha, Sesshomaru & Koga: In an action-packed scene, the two half-brothers are battling a common foe with their trusty swords as Koga swirls through the background, jaws agape and ready for some serious mauling.

Sesshomaru: An extremely cool-looking Sesshomaru holds Tenseiga thrust out before him as lightning crackles off the blade. In the background, the nighttime forest is awash in the blue glow of the full moon.

InuYasha & Sesshomaru: A color inkwash of InuYasha superimposed on a larger black and white illustration of Sesshomaru. Both half-brothers have their swords unsheathed, but InuYasha has his thrown back over his shoulder, as if he's contemplating the next stage of the story.

Movic $5.00

Kagome
—— Schoolgirl & Demon Fighter

InuYasha Profile 002
Name: Kagome Higurashi

Kagome is a schoolgirl in her third and final year of junior high school who lives in the modern day Higurashi Shrine. She enters a time warp through the well in the hall of the shrine, emerging in the Era of Warring States, where she meets InuYasha. She frees him from his spell by removing the hama no ya, the arrow that seals him in the sacred tree.

But the Shikon jewel that she has brought with her is stolen by the demon Shibugarasu, and is shattered into a million fragments when she shoots an arrow at the thieving demon in an attempt to stop him. The consequence of the shards of the jewel falling into the hands of the demons is too much to bear, so she sets out with InuYasha to recover as many of the pieces of the jewel as she can.

While Kagome is searching for the fragments of the Shikon jewel in ancient Japan, she is also leading the busy life of a junior high school student with high school entrance exams coming up.

It is also important to remember that Kagome is the reincarnation of Kikyo, the very miko priestess who sealed InuYasha up in the tree in the first place.

Kagome Higurashi was born and raised in Higurashi Shrine. There she lives with her grandfather, her mother, her younger brother Sota and her cat Buyo.

See Glossary
Buyo

There are many kinds of shrines in Japan that worship various gods. Japan is said to be a country of "8 million gods," although the term more comfortably translates to "many" or "a multitude" of deities.

The god worshipped at Higurashi Shrine is the sacred tree - literally, "the God Tree," which sits in the garden and is tightly bound with a sacred straw cord, or festoon, known as shimenawa. Also worshipped at Higurashi Shrine is the dry well in the hall - the one that Kagome enters the time warp through.

The fact that neither of these objects of worship is in anyway human is of no consequence in Japan, where the more animist beliefs endow natural features such as trees and boulders with god-like qualities.

Let's just take a minute here to discuss

how long this shrine has been around.

When Kagome emerges from the well in the Warring States period, it is clear that the well itself is there, and that the sacred tree in which InuYasha is imprisoned is also there. But there is no sign of the shrine itself.

Therefore the shrine was clearly built in a later period. When we consider that it is these two very elements that are the objects of worship in the modern day, we can surmise that it is because of what Kagome and InuYasha did and achieved that people now believe the tree and the well to be sacred. The shrine was obviously built later to worship them.

This supposition is reinforced when we consider that in many cases natural objects are endowed with sacred or god-like qualities after some kind of miraculous event. In this sense, the imprisonment and release of InuYasha from the sacred tree and the use of the well to slip back in time are equally miraculous.

In other words, the shrine was built there because of the activities of InuYasha, and the Higurashi family, from which the guardians of the shrine or the Shinto priests emerge, is connected to InuYasha. I personally believe they are related to the miko priestess Kaede. That would work to explain how Kagome could be the reincarnation of Kikyo.

See Glossary
InuYasha
Era of Warring
  States
Miko
Kaede
Kikyo

See questions
13

agome enters the hall in search of her cat Buyo. There she is attacked by the monster centipede Mukadejoro, causing her to fall into the well and through a time slip back to the Era of Warring States.

Later we discover that it's impossible to enter the time warp unless you are carrying the Shikon jewel, or fragments of it. The first time Kagome goes through the time warp she is bitten in the left side by Mukadejoro, and out pops the jewel. From this we realize she's been carrying it about inside her.

Let's also not forget that the jewel was buried along with Kikyo during the Warring States period. So, the fact that it now emerges from inside Kagome further establishes the idea that she is the reincarnation of Kikyo.

See Glossary

Buyo
Mukadejoro
Era of Warring States
Shikon jewel
Kikyo

See questions
12

The secret behind the name "Kagome"

Young Japanese children sometimes sing a song called "Kagome-Kagome". They form a circle holding hands. One child stands in the center and covers his eyes with his hands. The circle starts to rotate, while the children sing, "Kagome Kagome/Kago no naka no tori wa/Itsu itsu deyaru?/Yoake to ban ni/Tsuru to kame ga subetta/Ushiro no shomen dare?"

A rough translation of this is "Kagome, Kagome/When oh when/Will the caged bird be released?/At the first light of dawn and twilight/And when the turtle and the crane slip and fall/Who is it who is directly behind you?"

There appears to be no real meaning to the lyrics, although they may date back to the Edo period. If asked, who is this Kagome, most Japanese would be unable to reply.

One answer is in the direct translation of "kagome" - "the eyes of the basket" - meaning the many apertures produced when weaving a basket. There is one theory that these "eyes" work to protect us, by glaring back at the evil spirits that surround us in our daily lives.

If that is the case, then "Kagome" is the perfect name for a miko priestess, with all her spiritual powers.

14 Just what is the Shikon jewel, and why is it so important?

The "four souls" of the Shikon jewel are Aramitama - the guardian of courage; Nigimitama - the guardian of affinity; Kushimitama - the guardian of knowledge; and Sachimitama - the guardian of love. When all these four spirits are in harmony, they create a power balance called Naohi.

This jewel has unique powers that can endow the user with miraculous capabilities. The monster centipede that appears in the first episode normally takes the form of a creature with the upper body of a woman and a centipede's lower body. But once the centipede has swallowed the jewel it morphs into something akin to a turbocharged alien.

The demon-bird Shibugarasu also normally looks like any other bird. But with the jewel, it morphs into a monster.

The jewel also works its magic on humans. Kohaku, the younger brother of Sango, was brought back from the dead after being implanted with a shard of the jewel.

See Glossary
Shikon jewel
Shibugarasu
Kohaku
Demon
Sango

There is also the case of Nikutsuki no Men - the mask of flesh. Carved from the trunk of an ancient tree that had a shard of the jewel embedded in it, the mask attaches itself to its victims and cannot be removed until the unfortunate person dies.

See Glossary
Nikutsuki no Men
Kotatsu
Kikyo
Era of Warring States

There is the painter Kotatsu, who mixes shards of the jewel into his paint when he depicts demons. As a result, the images spring to life. In other words, all things in creation can benefit from the power of the jewel.

Still, such objects endowed with wonderful powers are also prone to be abused, especially if they fall into the hands of evil, such as demons.

This is why it was necessary for Kikyo, with her spiritual strength and stoic's lifestyle, to control what was potentially such a dangerous talisman. It is significant that she takes the jewel with her to the grave.

Kikyo reappears in the Era of Warring States in the form of Kagome, and it is with the single shot of an arrow released by Kagome that the jewel shatters and is dispersed throughout the land. Even broken into a million pieces the jewel loses none of its powers, and is soon abused when falling into the hands of demons. Everyone wants the jewel for their own purposes; the demon Naraku - the nemesis of InuYasha - wants the fragments so he can become the almighty demon; InuYasha - a demi-demon - wants the pieces so he can become a full-blooded demon; and poor Kagome - the schoolgirl from the future - is driven by her sense of guilt at being the one responsible for shattering the jewel into a million shards.

It suffices to say that without the existence of the Shikon jewel there would be no InuYasha. That's how important it is to the story.

See Glossary
Naraku
InuYasha

See questions
15 **16** **30** **33**

15 Why is it that only Kagome can see each individual fragment of the jewel?

We see that the Shikon jewel loses none of its positive spiritual power, even after it is shattered. And while such characters as InuYasha, Miroku and Sango are extremely sensitive to the powers of evil - allowing them to sense when a demon is close by - they are not well tuned to positive spiritual power.

On the other hand, Kagome can sense the powers of good as well as those of evil, and this allows her - and her alone - to sense if a fragment of the jewel is close by. It's not clear whether this is because she is the reincarnation of Kikyo, or because she is a miko priestess, but the fact is she is the only one in the entire story of InuYasha capable of sensing and seeing the fragments of the jewel.

S ee Glossary
Shikon jewel
InuYasha
Miroku
Sango
Kikyo
Miko

See questions
2 14 16 30

16 When was the Shikon jewel created?

It is said that the Shikon jewel was made during the Heian period when the nobility was at its peak.

There was a powerful miko priestess called Midoriko in the same village as the demon-exterminators. Legend had it that she could dispose of ten demons at once with her spiritual powers. The demons try to get rid of Midoriko. Several demons possessed a man who harbored evil thoughts toward the miko, producing one gigantic demon that then confronted Midoriko.

The fight lasted three days and three nights, but in the end they destroyed each other. However, before they perished Midoriko sucked up the demon's spirit and locked it deep inside her own soul. It was this, ejected from Midoriko's body, that became the jewel of the four spirits.

Although the fight between Midoriko and the demons appeared to be over, it is in fact still raging within the jewel, with the exuding

See Glossary
Shikon jewel
Miko
Midoriko
Demon
Exterminators

powers combining to create an overwhelming energy. This leads to miraculous powers, regardless of whether they are used for good or for evil.

Later we see the jewel emerge from the body of a demon slain by Sango's grandfather. He entrusts it to Kikyo - the greatest of the living miko - hoping she can cleanse it of the evil it exudes. The jewel then passes into the body of Kagome following the death of Kikyo, returning to the Warring States period when Kagome goes through the time warp.

See Glossary
Sango
Kikyo

See questions
2 13 14 15

17 What kind of arrow is the hama no ya unleashed by Kagome?

Hama no ya - or "arrow of purity" - is not a specific weapon with a set shape or size. It is a charmed arrow with spiritual powers aimed at exterminating demons.

Such arrows have long been sold in shrines throughout Japan, and are purchased by worshippers over the New Year period to be placed in family altars to ward off evil spirits, bad luck and unhappiness over the coming year.

It follows that if the arrow is unleashed by a miko priestess with the spiritual powers of someone like Kagome, then those powers pass into the arrow, which is then capable of inflicting damage to any evil presence - such as a demon.

This also explains why arrows with no specific spiritual powers used by ordinary human - beings that Kagome and InuYasha meet along the way - take on powers when they come into contact with Kagome. It is not so much a case of the arrow being sacred, but of

See Glossary
Demon
Miko
InuYasha

the sacred power in the miko being invested in the arrow, which then obliterates the evil power it is opposing.

When she first passed through the time warp, Kagome's powers were undeveloped. This meant that the arrows she released were not that potent. It is from midway through the adventure that her arrows take on bright, shining spiritual powers, heightening their ability to exterminate demons.

See questions
18

Kagome has clearly acquired a number of special qualities from her close association with Kikyo - she is after all the reincarnation of this powerful miko priestess.

First of all she has the strange powers associated with the spiritual force of the charmed arrows, which allows her to gather any number of powers into the palm of her hand, and then direct them at an opponent with great destructive power. This is the power she musters unconsciously when attacked by Mukadejoro, or Mistress Centipede.

Kagome also uses genkei jutsu to nullify the power of the apparitions and illusions that Naraku uses as a fighting technique. Kagome appears to be able to cleanse the evil from the very air around her, even as Miroku and Sango suffer under a mist-like shroud of wickedness.

Last but not least, let's not forget that as she is sucked through the time warp, Kagome seizes on an ordinary modern-day first-aid box, which she takes with her to the Warring States period, and which allows her to play the role of nurse.

See Glossary
Kikyo
Miko
Mukadejoro
Naraku
Miroku
Sango

See questions
17

InuYasha Cell Phone Cover

Bandai, that fine purveyor of tie-in toys, has released a whole series of anime art for cell phones. Known as Chara Haru Art, the series would not be replete without InuYasha.

The concept is simple, and applying the design is easier than it looks. The kit consists of one colored transparent sheet and some clear tape. Simply cut the sheet and place one part over the outside of the phone, smooth it with your fingers and adhere with the tape. Any rough edges can be removed with a sharp knife.

Once that's complete, do the same for the inside of the phone. Cover the screen and push-buttons, stick and cut. The actual material is so clear and pliable that it doesn't affect visuals or working the number board. In fact, the artwork acts more like a wrapper, tightly encasing the phone so that it looks like it's been on there forever.

We chose the purple design, with InuYasha and Kagome on the back falling through the well. Emblazoned on the front are the InuYasha kanji characters. However, there are others designs in blossom pink and aquamarine that depict different characters and InuYasha striking other poses.

Bandai
$15.00

19 Kagome seems to spend all her time going back and forth between the two periods. Does she still make it to school every day?

Even while off on her demon-repelling, jewel-seeking adventures, Kagome does not put herself out in her daily life, and although we cannot say she makes it on time every day, she does occasionally attend class.

Still, there's not much you can do if you're the reincarnation of one of the most powerful miko priestesses who ever lived, and are sucked through a time warp. School tends to end up being less important.

See Glossary
Miko
Hojo

Kagome's granddad comes up with an encyclopedia of assumed illnesses that prevent Kagome from going to school. This is so effective that even her classmates believe Kagome to be a weak, sickly child, and are very considerate to her on the occasions she does make it to class.

There is a boy in her class called Hojo who likes Kagome and is concerned for her health. He sometimes gives her presents such as health sandals, which are supposed to promote physical activity by stimulating the pressure points.

Of course, if she walked around telling everyone she had just returned from the Era of Warring States they'd think she'd gone soft in the head. So it's not something she shouts around town.

Her family - possibly because they live in a shrine with all its connotations of spirits, mystery and miracles - accept the incredible things she says as just another part of their own spiritual world. It is because of the understanding of her family that she is able to continue her split existence between the modern and the Warring States periods.

See Glossary
Era of Warring States

See questions
13

See Glossary

InuYasha
Demon
Kikyo
Shikon jewel
Urasue

We know that InuYasha is a demi-demon born of a demon father who fell in love with a human woman, so it is not that strange that InuYasha does as his father did and fall in love with a mortal. That woman is Kikyo, and it is for her sake that he forswears the demonic world and looks to use the Shikon jewel to become a full-fledged human being.

It is only natural therefore that he feels drawn to Kagome, who is the reincarnation of his old flame. But Kagome is jealous of this significant other in InuYasha's life, and wants to be loved for herself, not as the alter ego of a past love.

Kikyo herself reappears thanks to the magic of Urasue, creating the strangest of ménage a trois. Hey, one of these women is the reincarnation of the other, and that significant other has just been raised from the dead! What's the problem?

Still, Kikyo must return to the grave, and

InuYasha must go with her if her chooses Kikyo over Kagome. It's a question of love and live, or love and die...which is probably why he chooses Kagome.

There is a strong possibility this love will bear fruit. But if it does, then they have to decide whose house they will live in - one in the modern period or one in the Era of Warring States.

And it is perhaps significant that when they have their lover's quarrels Kagome threatens to return to her parent's house. It is tradition in Japan for a bride to leave the house of her parents and become a member of her husband's family upon marriage. But if they separate, she returns to her parent's home. So by saying this, Kagome may be suggesting that she has decided to stay with InuYasha in the Warring States period...but only if things go well in their relationship.

See questions
4 30

Miroku
— Buddhist Monk & Ladies Man

InuYasha Profile 003
Name: Miroku

Miroku is a Buddhist monk. As a result of a curse placed on his grand-father by Naraku, he is born with a hole, sometimes referred to as a "wind hole," in his right hand - a kind of black hole that sucks in everything around it. This hole works to drain the life from Miroku himself, and it is just a question of time before he himself is sucked into its vortex. It is also a powerful weapon if used properly.

The family of Miroku has spent three generations hunting down Naraku, so Miroku throws in his lot with InuYasha when he hears he is also searching for the demon.

Because of his many years of Buddhist training, he is able to make a cool and dispas-sionate analysis of the situation and arrive at a suitable plan of action, unlike the more impul-sive demi-demon InuYasha.

As such, it would be convenient to call him the brains of the operation. But despite all this meditative dis-cipline and casting off of the material world, his major failing is earthbound - he has sex on the brain and can't keep away from the ladies.

21 What does Miroku do as a Buddhist monk?

As a Buddhist monk, Miroku would be expected to both preach the Buddha's law and live by it. He can be expected to have studied the teachings of the Buddha through the scriptures in an attempt to achieve enlightenment.

His main task is to guide others towards similar enlightenment and ensure that the souls of the dead attain their rightful place in the afterlife to become Buddhas.

There are those spirits that for some reason do not proceed directly to the afterlife, and therefore cannot achieve Buddha-hood. Instead, they linger on in this world to haunt the living as vengeful ghosts or evil spirits. In this case, Miroku would be expected to exorcise the evil in them by preaching the word of the Buddha and setting the spirits back on the road to attaining enlightenment.

Miroku would be based in a temple from where he would carry out his work. This differs to the family of Kagome, who, because

See Glossary
Miroku

they are believers in the more animistic, ancestor-worshipping Shinto religion, live in a shrine.

In modern day Japan, the two religions harmoniously overlap, with events such as birth and marriage generally given over to Shinto rituals, and those of death to Buddhism.

Throughout the series we come across scenes of Miroku burying the remains of those killed by demons, and even of dead demons themselves, while also performing meditation so that their souls may pass to the afterlife. This is in line with the Buddhist belief that death is the great equalizer, bringing everyone to the same level. Even those who committed acts of great evil in their lives will be afforded the same rituals as the righteous.

We can see that much of Miroku's work is to do with the dead, and that he is highly skilled in exorcising evil spirits - normally by chanting the scriptures, the powerful drone of which drives away evil elements.

The question remains: does Buddhist ritual work on demons? Miroku himself is both an exorcist in the western and Christian sense of the word, but he is also a proficient hand-to-hand fighter...not something regularly seen in Buddhist monks.

See Glossary
Demon

See questions
1

22 How does Miroku end up with the hole in his right hand?

The hole in Miroku's right hand is the result of a curse by Naraku...but for that story we have to go back half a century. Some 50 years ago, Miroku's grandfather was just seconds away from sealing up Naraku with a ritual tag, after finally tracking him down in an attempt to exterminate him, when the demon shot him through both tag and hand to escape.

As he is running away, Naraku says, "In time that hole in your hand will swallow you up as well. And as long as I am alive, that curse will be passed on to each and every one of your descendants."

He is true to his word. The black hole is passed on down through the generations, and both Miroku's grandfather and his father end up being sucked into the expanding vortex. The hole is also in Miroku's hand, and he could too get sucked in at any moment.

The only way to break the curse is to exterminate Naraku, who becomes his lifelong foe. And it is while searching down the source of the curse that he runs into InuYasha et al.

See Glossary
Kazana
Miroku
Naraku
InuYasha

See questions
23

So what of Miroku hoshi?

Miroku is known as the Buddhist god of compassion or benevolence. In Buddhism, only those who undergo meditative discipline will attain the position of gods - or Buddhas. Miroku is said to have undergone the necessary strictures and to have attained the same level as a god.

The Shingon sect - founded by Kobo Daishi - believes Miroku is destined to return as a Buddha after 5.67 billion years and save all those who have failed to achieve enlightenment.

23 What is the power of the hole in Miroku's right hand?

The hole has terrible powers and can suck in anything regardless of its size from hundreds of meters away. It would suck in a thousand demons all at once and hurl them off into a different dimension if Miroku were to use it in a fight.

Even though Naraku has put curse on Miroku, he fears the hole as a weapon even more so than InuYasha's sword Tessaiga.

But even the hole has weaknesses. First of all, it cannot choose what it sucks into its vortex. This means it is almost impossible to use in a fight where friends and foes are all in together. Also, the object to be sucked into the vortex must be in front of the hole and not behind it.

The hole's major adversaries are the Saimyosho - poisonous insect demons released by Naraku. They are about the size of bees but carry deadly poison that, if sucked into the hole, can poison Miroku, leaving him unable to move for days and close to death.

See Glossary

Kazana
Demon
Miroku
Naraku
InuYasha
Tessaiga
Saimyosho

Naraku, who of course knows only too well the power of the hole, invariably appears in front of Miroku with his Saimyosho. There is also a case where a praying mantis is sucked into the hole, but flicked out before being sucked into the vortex, making the hole even bigger and causing endless problems for Miroku.

Miroku normally seals the hole with prayer beads. These are linked on a cord and wrapped around the hand like a rosary. They become one of Miroku's tools and assume a sacred power of their own.

See Glossary
Juzu (Beads)

See questions
22

24 What is the hama no fuda that Miroku occasionally uses?

Miroku occasionally throws small scrolls of paper at the demons. These are known as hama no fuda. They are printed with extracts of Buddhist scripture or curses that, when combined with the spirit that Miroku endows each individual scroll with, can cause damage to demons or objects mired in evil. The scrolls have the same power as chanting the Buddhist sutras, which have sacred powers that work to cleanse evil.

S ee Glossary
Miroku
Demon
Miko

The power of which we talk here is a power bestowed by the Buddha. It is not the mysterious, spiritual power of a miko priestess, but one which can be obtained through the disciplines of being a monk and understanding the teachings of the Buddha, although to master the most powerful requires vast efforts.

Miroku does not only hurl these prayer scrolls at demons like ninja shuriken. He also can remove the power of a curse by applying an unrolled scroll against the forehead of someone who has been cursed.

Besides from hama no fuda, Miroku sometimes uses mayoke no gofu - charms to ward off evil. These are imprinted with spells or words that demons fear and despise. Demons can be chased out of or warded away from houses by affixing the charm to the main pillar or column of the structure.

Miroku is known to use this for his own personal benefit, especially as night falls and he must find a place to stay. He often approaches the most affluent looking home in the area and declares, "There are demons in this house!" He then proceeds to chase them out by affixing scrolls to the main column running through the center of the dwelling. He generally claims something highly valuable or a bed for the night as payment for this unselfish act - even if, as is often the case, there are no demons present at all.

25 *What is the cane that Miroku carries with him?*

Miroku carries a monk's cane with him at all times. This is supposed to help him as he negotiates hills and rough terrain, and was never originally intended to be used for fighting. The staff has six interlocking rings of various sizes near the handle that jingle as he walks, announcing his presence to those nearby and at the same time warding off evil.

Having sworn himself to tracking down Naraku, Miroku has mastered numerous martial arts. But he also uses his staff as a weapon. The stick is endowed with vast spiritual powers, and is strong enough to repel even the sword Tessaiga. The bodies of mere demons are no match for such a powerful weapon.

See Glossary

Miroku
Naraku
Tessaiga
Demon

See questions

9

InuYasha Pencils

Mitsubishi, which does everything from auto-making to banking, also makes pencils - InuYasha pencils no less!

If you want to practice your kanji-writing, or are a budding mangaka, then these are just the thing for you.

In a box emblazoned with your favorite InuYasha characters are 12 six-sided pencils, down which of each are the six main characters and InuYasha in big blue kanji.

Not merely pencils, these writing tools are specially designed to allow you to write clearly and without getting hand strain. Believe it or not, on the back of the box are long and in-depth instructions on how to get the most of your InuYasha pencils.

Advice includes: How to write without growing tired; How to hold your pencil in the correct manner; and How to write concisely. This must be Japan!

Mitsubishi
$6.00
© Takahashi Rumiko/
Shogakkan/
Yomiuri TV/Sunrise 2000

26 What is it with Miroku and the opposite sex?

Miroku has more chat-up lines than an escort service, and goes into testosterone-fueled overdrive whenever he comes into contact with the fairer sex. He takes every chance he can to fondle Sango's derriere, and has angered the women in the InuYasha group, such as Kagome and Sango, with such sweet-talk as, "How about having my baby?"

At first sight, a set of chromosomes with "one-track-mind" written all over it seems to be embedded deep within the DNA of the Miroku family. It is said that Miroku's grandfather got the hole in his hand when he dropped his guard as Naraku appeared before him in the form of an enticing young woman.

At the same time, though, there may be some justification for his line, "How about having my baby?" Let's not forget that the curse of the hole threatens to suck in Miroku himself, and that he can count the years he has left to live on one hand - pun not intended.

Given that Miroku is the third genera-

See Glossary
Miroku
Sango
InuYasha
Naraku
Kazana

tion that has tried to track down Naraku - and that both his father and his grandfather failed - it is reasonable to think that Miroku has accepted the likelihood that he too may not succeed in the quest, and is planning ahead for the next generation, placing his hopes on a child.

Naraku cursed Miroku's grandfather: "In time that hole in your hand will swallow you up as well. And as long as I am alive that curse will be passed on to each and every one of your descendants." Needless to say, Miroku is not going to take this lying down - not alone at least - and is going to do everything he can to make sure he has a child who can carry on where he leaves off.

See questions
22

27 Who is Mushin, who raised Miroku?

Miroku's father was swallowed up by the hole in his hand right before Miroku's young eyes, leaving only the hole, which is kept under safe keeping at the temple overseen by Mushin. Losing his father in this way was a shock for Miroku, who reacted by becoming a rebellious kid.

It was Mushin who gave him encouragement, and trained him to be a monk. Mushin is not your typical by-the-scripture-monk. He drinks in the middle of the day, and sleeps it off when he should be working. But the fact of the matter is that he is the only one who can take care of the hole in Miroku's hand.

It was Mushin that Miroku went to for help when a praying mantis opened the vent in his hand wider than it was before. And he depends on him for a lot in the absence of his own father.

See Glossary
Miroku
Kazana
Mushin

See questions
22 28

71

InuYasha Pencil Caps

If you've already bought the InuYasha pencils, but find you can't stop chewing the tops off of them, then these pencils caps are just the ticket.

In two colors - pink and purple - are five InuYasha pencil caps depicting that cute two-tailed feline demon Kirara and Shippo above him. There are numerous variations available, including the two half-brothers, InuYasha and Sesshomaru; Miroku and his soon-to-be sweetheart Sango; and Kagome and her own cat Buyo.

Fitting any standard-size pencil, these caps are made from thick plastic that'll put a stop to any gnawing.

Sakamoto Co., Ltd.
$1.50
© Takahashi Rumiko/
Shogakkan/
Yomiuri TV/Sunrise 2000

28 Is Miroku as bad a monk as some people make out?

Let's go back and talk a little about that rebellious phase that Miroku went through. At one stage he pounced on poor Jaken - the reptilian-like follower of Sesshomaru - with murder in his eyes. And later on we see that Miroku's friend Hachiemon the tanuki - a raccoon-like animal - is also afraid of Miroku's violent streak.

We also know that Miroku takes advantage of his position as a monk, especially when as night arrives he finds himself with no place to stay. He "offers" his services as an exorcist to the most affluent looking family in the area, claiming valuables as payment - even if there are no demons to be exorcised.

Miroku has accepted his lot in life, and is determined to track down Naraku, but we should not forget that there are times when his actions suggest that he is a bad monk.

S ee Glossary
Miroku
Jaken
Sesshomaru
Naraku
Demon

See questions
27 29

29 What is the demon tanuki that is often with Miroku?

The demon tanuki that Miroku is often with has the very long name of Awanohachiemondanuki (usually known as Hachiemon the tanuki). He has been at the beck and call of the monk from way back. Hachiemon has only the barest of demon capabilities and is no use whatsoever when it comes to a fight.

Apart from coming to his master's aid in times of trouble, he is also useful for his ability to change his appearance. He conjures himself up into something resembling a gigantic hot air balloon that he uses to ship Miroku off to distant places.

Hachiemon's trademark line is the oft repeated - "Master Miroku! Just give me a break!" Considering Miroku's violent streak, when together they give the appearance not so much as master and servant, but gang leader and gofer. The tanuki must have taken a few knocks when Miroku was going through his rebellious phase. But we can also see there is a friendship of sorts between them.

See Glossary
Demon
Miroku

See questions
28

Kikyo
—Priestess & Significant Other

InuYasha Profile 004
Name: Kikyo

Kikyo is the only one with the spiritual powers to cleanse and control the Shikon jewel. She falls in love with InuYasha, who pledges to use the jewel to become fully human so that he can live out his days with her. But she believes, falsely, that InuYasha has betrayed her. She is hurt both physically and emotionally, and dies after sealing InuYasha in the sacred tree.

She is brought back to life by Urasue, and appears before InuYasha on several occasions as she attempts to guide him to the afterlife. She has lost none of her powers, and even the evil Naraku thinks twice about meddling with her.

30 How is it that Kikyo came to control the Shikon jewel?

During the Warring States period, Kikyo was famed throughout the land as the miko priestess with the most advanced spiritual powers.

When Sango's father, after exterminating a demon, acquired the Shikon jewel, he knew only too well of its dangers. He therefore asked Kikyo to look after it. Kikyo lived up to his expectations by cleansing the jewel of its evil properties, and keeping it close by her so no one else could abuse its properties.

See Glossary
Kikyo
Miko
Sango's father
Shikon jewel
Demon
InuYasha

But looking after the jewel appears to have taken its toll on Kikyo's mental state. At one stage she reveals that the burden of the job has left her leading the life of a stoic, when she tells InuYasha, "I cannot stray from my purpose and must never show any sign of weakness, because the demons will immediately take advantage of it. I am human, and yet not so. InuYasha! We are two of a kind, and I am closer to you - the demi-demon - than you care to think."

InuYasha sympathizes with her plight, and it is not long before they develop affection for each other. So Kikyo decides to use the jewel to help InuYasha. She realizes this will help release her from her lonesome existence, as the jewel will disappear after being thoroughly cleansed and helping InuYasha become human.

It is said that a miko loses her spiritual powers once she has pledged herself to a particular man. So by doing this for InuYasha, it is likely that Kikyo is prepared to give up her role as a miko priestess. But Naraku manages to take advantage of this moment of weakness and the future turns out very different.

See Glossary
Naraku

See questions
1 **2**

31 What is the plot that Naraku weaves around Kikyo?

Naraku has been plotting to get his hands on the Shikon jewel in Kikyo's care for the last 50 years. But he doesn't just want the jewel as it is. He wants it brimming with evil power, and so tries to imprint upon Kikyo's pure heart bitter feelings of hatred and resentment.

For her part, Kikyo is in love with InuYasha, and is looking for ways to use the jewel to make him become totally human so they can be married. InuYasha feels the same way.

Naraku does everything he can to come between them. He appears before Kikyo in the form of InuYasha and pours scorn upon her, saying, "Human? I never once intended to become human!" He then attacks her before making off with the jewel.

Naraku also manages to pull the wool over InuYasha's eyes, maneuvering to make him seize the jewel for himself. And it is probably by poisoning the hearts of both Kikyo and

See Glossary
Naraku
Shikon jewel
Kikyo
InuYasha

InuYasha with bitterness that Naraku hopes to make the jewel resonate with evil.

But Naraku does not get his way. Kikyo uses the last of her strength to chase down InuYasha and seal him up in the sacred tree. With her last act on earth, she manages to cleanse the jewel before dying. The jewel is buried with her and disappears, only to reemerge with Kagome - the reincarnation of Kikyo.

See questions
14 15 16

32 Why is Kikyo brought back to life?

The Shikon jewel exerts a powerful pull over all demons. Urasue, who uses the remains of the dead to bring them back to life so as to exert control over them, steals Kikyo's remains in order to reanimate her so the miko priestess will tell her the whereabouts of the jewel.

Urasue manages to resuscitate Kikyo's body, but her soul has already been transferred to her reincarnation, Kagome, and Kikyo lies there like a clay figure with no power to move. Urasue tries to suck the soul of Kikyo out of Kagome and replace it in its original body, but fails.

For her part, Kikyo clings to the chance to live again, and manages to reconstitute herself by gathering together the souls of other dead people. She resigns herself to existing on earth as one of the living dead, although with a will of her own.

In the Warring States period, those like Kikyo who died with feelings of hatred, resent-

See Glossary
Shikon jewel
Demon
Urasue
Kikyo
Miko

ment and revenge would become avenging spirits, destined to bring unhappiness to all they came into contact with. In an attempt to offset this, the living would provide such spirits with offerings.

Kikyo becomes such an avenging spirit, despite the fact that her grave is not simply decorated with a stone to mark the spot, but has a grand hall built around it in an attempt to soothe her angry spirit.

See questions
14

Because Kikyo's true soul now resides in Kagome's body, she is forced to use as her life energy the souls of young dead women brought to her by a demon called Shinidamachu - the soul collector. He serves Kikyo as a servant or retainer after she comes back to life.

See Glossary
Kikyo
Demon
Shinidamachu
Shikon jewel

If we compare the characters of Kikyo and Kagome - Kikyo's reincarnation - we can see that while Kikyo is extremely reserved, never giving expression to her feelings, Kagome is a simple and innocent girl who gives full flight to her feelings - crying when she is sad, laughing when she is happy, and capable of telling those she has feelings for, "I love you."

But these surely are the true feelings that Kikyo herself would have felt deep down inside. Kikyo could have been full of life - her reserved nature is the result of forcefully keeping a lid on her vitality while taking on the burden of protecting the Shikon jewel.

When Kikyo comes back to life she is

freed from that burden, and can be true to her feelings once again. She no longer has to hide her love for InuYasha, and is able to give full expression to her feelings - she kisses InuYasha - and gives vent to an anger she was forced to suppress while alive. And what's more, she enjoys this newfound freedom! She says, "I feel that this is the real me!"

In other words, it is not that Kikyo's character changes after she comes back from the dead, but instead that she is released from her obligation to lead a stoic lifestyle. She is given the chance to enjoy life, even though she is now one of the living dead!

See Glossary
InuYasha

34 What is Kikyo's purpose in lingering on in the Era of Warring States?

The newly liberated Kikyo burns with the desire to strike down Naraku, who she now realizes cheated her, and to take the man she loved - InuYasha - into the afterlife to be with her forever.

But she is unable to kill InuYasha, even though, as an avenging spirit, it would be the easiest thing in the world. She even gives Naraku some of the shards of the Shikon jewel that she has taken from Kagome.

Why she can do one and not the other remains something of a mystery, and we are not clear as to what her true aim is in this new life.

ee Glossary
Kikyo
Naraku
InuYasha
Shikon jewel

See questions
20

Kikyo, Kaede, Sango... secrets, secrets, secrets...

Many of the female characters in InuYasha have been given flower names. These are not simply proper names, but metaphors for emotions or mental states represented by specific flowers. For example, "kikyo" translates as a Chinese bellflower, or balloon flower, which blooms with purple and white flowers and represents sincerity.

This all ties in with another quasi-religious belief prevalent in Japan of old, kotodama shinko - the belief that words were not used merely to convey meaning, but were talismans expressing spiritual or higher states of mind. It was believed that beautiful, correct words brought about good, and that words of the opposite kind caused evil.

Under this old set of beliefs a name was used not only to represent the person, but upon utterance became the very person him- or herself. To know someone's name was to know everything about them, and be capable of stealing their soul.

That is why women in particular were wary of anyone knowing their names. Apart from her immediate family, the only person a woman would reveal her name to was the man she intended to marry. It was considered taboo for anyone else to refer to her by that name.

Women in particular employed a series of titles for use in everyday life. These might be called nicknames today, but may have been connected with her appearance, her station in life or her parent's occupation. This is true of the men of the time as well, who often went by role-based names. Outside the immediate family the name a person was born with might never be revealed until his death. Indeed, the word for someone's real name - imina - literally means, "taboo name." Women used aza, or assumed names.

This helps explain the euphonious sounding names used in InuYasha, such as Kikyo (balloon flower), Kaede (maple leaf) and Sango (coral). All are assumed names.

Sesshomaru
—— Half-Brother & Cool Killer

InuYasha Profile 005
Name: Sesshomaru

Sesshomaru is the elder half-brother of InuYasha. He is born of a demon mother, which makes him a demon full-blood, unlike InuYasha. There is no love lost between the two brothers, especially as the demi-demon InuYasha is considered to be the source of family shame.

In particular, Sesshomaru is not happy that his father has left Tessaiga to InuYasha. Not only does he consider Tessaiga to be a superior sword to Tenseiga, the sword his father left him, but he also believes it his rightful inheritance, and he attacks InuYasha in order to seize the Tenseiga.

One other major difference between the brothers is that Sesshomaru shows almost no interest in gathering together the shards of the Shikon jewel - he considers that as a demon full-blood he is strong enough without it.

35 If Sesshomaru's so tough, why is he obsessed with Tessaiga?

We know that Sesshomaru takes great pride in believing that he, like his father before him, is the strongest demon around. So it follows that as Tessaiga is the epitome of sword craftsmanship, and the meanest piece of metal around, Sesshomaru sees it as his birthright.

Demons are unable to touch Tessaiga, and Sesshomaru has never been allowed to hold it in his hand. But forbidden fruit is the sweetest, and even though he considers himself strong enough without the sword, Sesshomaru would think nothing of killing his half-brother InuYasha to get his hands on it.

But if it's not about the sword, and it's not about amassing greater power, then what is Sesshomaru's hang up?

Sesshomaru cannot stomach the fact that by leaving Tessaiga, with its ability to kill 100 demons with a single sweep, to InuYasha, his father has anointed his half-blood brother as the rightful heir to the family name.

See Glossary
Sesshomaru
Tessaiga
Demon
InuYasha

The root of all this discord is envy over the fact that their father showed more love for InuYasha than for Sesshomaru. The attacks that Sesshomaru launches on InuYasha are as much about exhibiting his strength and showing who is top dog as they are about seizing the sword.

While on the surface, Sesshomaru may come across as strong, cruel and aloof, in reality he still has some readjusting to make before he becomes fully adult. For the moment, he remains immature and confused.

See questions 3 9

36 Just how tough is Sesshomaru then?

s has been mentioned already, Sesshomaru takes great pride in believing he is the strongest there is. He doesn't need to go off on some hare-brained caper to seek the fragments of any damned jewel, or so he thinks.

Apart from exhibiting extreme power in direct attacks, his killer technique is the Dokkaso - poisonous claw attack - by which he releases poison through the tips of his claws to melt his opponents while he tears them apart. He also shares InuYasha's heightened sense of smell, and is able to instantly tell what is happening a great distance away.

Sesshomaru has also inherited from his father the ability to morph into a huge dog, and it is in this form that he exhibits the most strength. Still, he seldom takes on this appearance as he has yet to meet an opponent worthy of his full power.

Sesshomaru exudes enough evil to effectively nullify the evil qualities of those around

See Glossary
Sesshomaru
InuYasha

him. He is so full of venom that he is able to shake off the poison emanating from the cursed sword Tokijin, which was made from one of the fangs of Goshinki by evil swordsmith Kajinbo.

He has honed his battle senses, and while it took InuYasha some time to master Tessaiga's Bakuryuha technique, Sesshomaru senses instantly that it is based on kaze no kizu, and is able to set it in motion the moment he picks it up. (I know we said demons cannot even touch Tessaiga. So, what's all this about Sesshomaru picking it up and acting like it was his own, you ask? He used a human hand to pick up Tessaiga!)

See Glossary

Tokijin
Tessaiga
Kaze no kizu
Goshinki
Kajinbo

See questions
6 **7** **9** **35**

37 What kind of sword is Tenseiga?

See Glossary
Tessaiga
Tenseiga
Sesshomaru
InuYasha
Totosai
Demon

Like Tessaiga, Tenseiga was made from the fangs of the father of Sesshomaru and InuYasha and beaten into a sword by the sword smith Totosai.

But while Tessaiga is said to be capable of killing 100 demons in a single swipe, Tenseiga is said to have the healing qualities capable of saving 100 lives. Perhaps that's why Sesshomaru has no use for the sword, preferring something that can defend its owner and kill his opponents.

The question is - why did his father leave Tenseiga to Sesshomaru?

Sesshomaru's father was probably deeply concerned that his son would become a victim of his own strength. He knew that his son could develop an increasingly cruel character that had no respect for the value of life; the type of demon that wouldn't think twice about snuffing out anyone that stood in his way.

His father wanted Sesshomaru to become a demon with the real ability to see that, "A man's true strength is not in taking life, but in giving it."

If this is the case, then by bequeathing Tessaiga to InuYasha, his father wanted to teach his younger son the importance of protecting others by wielding a sword that, "Exhibits its true strength only for those with the desire to protect and not just kill."

We know that InuYasha is a half-demon, and as a result is excluded from both demon and human worlds, made fun of by demon full-bloods, and never able to really get close to humans. This is why he develops a warped view of the world, deciding to go out there and take whatever he wants by sheer force and by relying on nobody.

In receiving Tessaiga, the lesson taught to InuYasha is that it is important to have something to protect in this world.

See questions
3 4 9 35
38

It is simply a case of give and take. Rin takes care of Sesshomaru when he is injured, and that's why he uses the healing powers of Tenseiga for the first time to bring her back to life after she is killed by a wolf.

See Glossary
Rin
Sesshomaru
Tenseiga

Rin sees her entire family murdered in front of her very eyes. As a result, she loses the ability to speak. She lives a solitary existence, but is forced to become one tough cookie, going out to steal vegetables from the fields in order to survive.

When this mute child tries her hardest to keep Sesshomaru alive, who is on the verge of death, emotions that he has never experienced before well up within him. He is grateful to her, but at the same time has pity for her, with her kindly smile and empty life.

By using Tenseiga for the reason it was originally intended - to save lives - he feels the joy of rescuing another human being and understands the value of human life.

Saving Rin sets off a change within

Sesshomaru. He begins to look on his demi-demon half-brother with the protective, encouraging eyes of an older brother. He even occasionally offers InuYasha advice. It's altogether different from the Sesshomaru that viewed his half-brother as the shame of the family and someone better off dead.

It is this change in Sesshomaru that adds to the appeal of the second half of the InuYasha saga. It causes us to think again about the foresight and wisdom of the man that fathered both Sesshomaru and InuYasha.

See Glossary
InuYasha

See questions
37

39 What kind of sword is Tokijin that Sesshomaru had Totosai's one-time assistant Kaijinbo forge for him?

Sesshomaru has Tokijin made so that he will have a weapon on a par with InuYasha's Tessaiga. The sword is forged from the fangs of Goshinki, which were powerful enough to break Tessaiga.

Kaijinbo was once Totosai's assistant, but Totosai cast him out of his workshop and disowned him after he discovered Kaijinbo was making nothing but evil swords and testing them by killing ten human beings with each one.

The evil-driven blacksmith forges Tokijin from the fangs of Goshinki, so there is an all-pervading aura of evil and ill-doing enveloping this new sword. And when Tokijin is complete, the evil it exudes sees its maker, Kaijinbo, go mad and rush to his death.

It is a backhanded tribute to Sesshomaru that his own aura of evil is so overpowering that it exceeds even that of Tokijin, setting him free from the risk of being used by the sword. But Tokijin, with its razor-sharp blade, is a destructive weapon in itself.

See Glossary

Sesshomaru
Tokijin
InuYasha
Tessaiga
Goshinki
Kaijinbo
Totosai

See questions
9 56

40 What kind of demon is Sesshomaru's sidekick, Jaken?

Jaken has known Sesshomaru's family for many years, and was probably recommended as a retainer by Sesshomaru and InuYasha's father.

He is a yes-man, who acts like a slave when he is around Sesshomaru, and will swallow any abuse whatsoever. His attitude, however, does a 180-degree flip when he is with other demons or humans, and he becomes a self-important, pompous, overweening, loud-mouthed boor.

In the presence of Sesshomaru he mouths platitudes and hollow praise, generally coming on like a Uriah Heep - very 'umble, very 'umble - but gets almost no praise from Sesshomaru in return.

Jaken is proud of Sesshomaru, and because of this his attempts to aid Sesshomaru are sincere. He carries a staff, called Nintojo (Staff of Heads), with two human faces on the end - a young girl's and an old man's. This Nintojo acts like radar when he is looking for something and as a flamethrower when he is on the attack.

⑤ee Glossary
Jaken
Sesshomaru
Demon
Nintojo
Aun

See questions
3 **11**

Naraku
—— Evil Incarnate & Super Demon

InuYasha Profile 006
Name: Naraku

Born out of a combination of demons, Naraku is InuYasha's arch-foe. It is perhaps fitting that someone named after Buddhism's hell should exude so much wickedness. In fact, anyone touching Naraku is likely to be poisoned. His aim in seeking out the pieces of the Shikon jewel is to contaminate the stone with his overwhelming evil and become the strongest demon alive. He has already accumulated a large number of the jewel's shards, and is growing stronger and stronger.

Naraku seldom goes into battle himself, using instead his alter ego, Kugutsu the puppet, and the demons Kagura, Kanna and Goshinki, which he has spawned from his own body. Naraku himself spends most of his time maneuvering and manipulating, looking to divide and conquer his enemies.

Naraku often appears in the form of the young lord of Hitomi Castle - Kagewaki Hitomi.

41 How did the evil Naraku come to exist?

Naraku is largely formed from the ugly thief Onigumo. Onigumo first appears bandaged from head to foot after being burnt. He is unable to do anything but lie on his back and talk. He is fed and cared for by Kikyo in a cave. But far from being grateful to Kikyo, Onigumo schemes to make her his woman.

Apart from his appalling appearance, which makes it unlikely Kikyo would ever be attracted to him, she has already fallen for InuYasha. At the same time, however, her feelings for InuYasha work to dilute her powers as a miko priestess, such as her ability to protect her village from demons.

For his part, Onigumo has set his warped heart of having Kikyo, and he concentrates his mind on communicating with the demons, telling them they can take over his body as long as he is able to move around. The demons manage to slip into the village under Kikyo's weakened "radar", and gather around the sick man.

See Glossary
Naraku
Onigumo
Kikyo
InuYasha
Miko
Demon

Onigumo tells them to eat his body so that his soul may occupy theirs. His wish is granted and the demons that eat of his body begin to combine. They are reborn as one evil entity with the soul of Onigumo. That moment sees the birth of Naraku.

This begs the question: Can demons normally combine at will in this way? The answer is, no. Demons may be monster-like beings with special abilities, but free combination is not one of them.

A very small number of demons have the ability to absorb other demons, becoming stronger with each new addition. Naraku is one, and all the demons in InuYasha are able to combine with this epitome of evil.

Rumiko Takahashi's concept of demons uniting to increase their strength may have been influenced by Go Nagai's Devilman. Devilman himself is the result of the unification of a demon and a human.

Devilman is recognized as a master-piece, and its carefully thought-out philosophical structure was well received both in Japan and overseas. The concept of demons combining may have influenced many other creators of manga and anime.

See questions
42 43 44 45
46 48

42 Is it true that InuYasha and Kikyo end up hating each other because of Naraku?

Naraku is made up mostly of evil demons, despite having the soul of the human being Onigumo. While Onigumo has surrendered his soul in order to get his hands on Kikyo, for the demons the first priority is to find all the shards of the Shikon jewel. This means that Naraku, first and foremost, wants to get his hands on the jewel. Kikyo is viewed as dispensable, especially if she gets in the way.

Naraku takes on the appearance of InuYasha to attack Kikyo, leaving her fatally wounded. His reason for doing so is to destroy the trust that exists between InuYasha and Kikyo and cause them to hate each other.

If things go according to Naraku's plans, Kikyo will use the jewel to grant her what she desires, corrupting the jewel in the process. Naraku then aims to kill Kikyo. But Kikyo makes no wish, instead taking the jewel with her to the grave. Naraku's plot fails, but the jewel is brought back by Kagome 50 years later. Again, Naraku sets his evil heart on obtaining it.

Ⓢee Glossary
Naraku
Demon
Onigumo
Kikyo
Shikon jewel
InuYasha

See questions
10 20 31

asha Teacup

Japanese tea will never go out of fashion. So it comes as no surprise to find that Movic has released a quality yu-nomi, or teacup, picturing the two half-brothers divided by Tessaiga in the foreground.

Sealed in a sturdy box, this lime-green cup is the ideal gift for any tea-loving anime fan. In a darker green line drawing, a relaxed InuYasha is pictured alongside his equally relaxed half-brother Sesshomaru. Thrust out provocatively before them is Tessaiga, as if tempting them to draw blood. For once, neither of them appear to dislike the other.

Beside each character are their names written in the kanji style we've all come to know so well.

Added touches included swirling clouds, blossom, leaves and crescent moons to make this quite a treasure for the InuYasha fan who thinks he or she has all the merchandise there is to have.

Movic
$8.00
© Takahashi Rumiko/
Shogakkan/
Yomiuri TV/Sunrise 2000

43 Is Naraku in fact Kagewaki Hitomi?

Although Naraku spends much of his time living in Hitomi Castle in the form of Kagewaki Hitomi, it doesn't mean that he is Hitomi. He is simply using Hitomi's body as a convenient receptacle.

We know that Naraku has the ability to take on the form of human beings. We have seen him do this when he appeared before Kikyo as InuYasha and attacked her. He also appears as a beautiful young woman, which causes Miroku's grandfather to lower his guard, allowing Naraku to open the black hole in his hand.

We also hear it directly from Miroku. At their very first meeting, he tells InuYasha, "My family has spent three generations searching for the demon Naraku, who can conceal himself by taking on any conceivable shape.

But what of the real Kagewaki Hitomi? A minor character in the InuYasha plot, Hitomi, as can be expected, is eventually murdered by Naraku.

See Glossary

Naraku
Kagewaki Hitomi
Kikyo
InuYasha
Miroku
Kazana
Demon

See questions

22 41 42

44 *What's the story behind the fur and mask that Naraku wears?*

Naraku appears wrapped in a white fur and a mask. It is believed to have come from a baboon demon. But the question is, why?

Apart from allowing him to conceal his identity, the fur is thought to have strong defensive powers. This represents Naraku's instincts for self-preservation, and explains why he seldom ventures into battle himself.

He may also be reliving some personality trait of Onigumo from deep within his subconscious. Let's not forget that Onigumo had a major complex about his ugliness. Naraku's desire to hide his true appearance beneath a fur may be the externalized expression of that complex.

See Glossary
Naraku
Onigumo

See questions
41

45 What is the spider-shaped scar on Naraku's back?

See Glossary
Naraku
Demon
Kagewaki
Hitomi
Onigumo
InuYasha

Naraku has a scar on his back that resembles a spider. The spider is the overriding external feature of the demon, even when he assumes the form of Kagewaki Hitomi. It is believed to be evidence that the soul of Onigumo - literally "demon spider" - continues to live on inside Naraku. Or, in reverse, that the badly burnt Onigumo continues to make his existence known to the physical world through the medium of the spider.

Naraku loathes this scar. Evil though he was, Onigumo was also fully human. What this means is that Naraku, while born of a combination of demons that took over Onigumo's body, is still part human.

Like InuYasha, Naraku is a demi-demon, and that bugs the hell out of him. He hates the spider mark because it is proof that he is less than a demon full-blood.

In an attempt to do away with the scar, he merges with other demons. But no matter how many times he undergoes this process, it

107

remains.

When Kikyo comes back to life, she immediately sees through Naraku because of his mark. "Demi-demon Naraku! You might think you have successfully changed into something nobody recognizes, but you will never remove the stain of Onigumo," she says. "That is why you seek the Shikon jewel, is it not? To become a demon full-blood."

She also provokes Naraku, telling him, "You will never be able to kill me!" And she is right. Naraku cannot kill Kikyo because she is the woman Onigumo fell for, and the soul of Onigumo is still alive deep within his subconscious.

We also know that Naraku tries to avoid meeting with InuYasha and his cohorts in battle, spending most of his time manipulating and maneuvering others to do his dirty work for him. This again may be Onigumo's defensive instincts rising to the surface.

As much as Naraku hates the human in Onigumo, it does allow him to drive a wedge between people because through Onigumo he knows their weaknesses.

See Glossary
Kikyo
Shikon jewel

See questions
31 41 44

46 Why is Naraku continually looking for demons to combine with?

Naraku continues to combine with various types of demons, not only in an attempt to wash away the mark of the spider from his demi-demon DNA, but also to acquire newer, superior powers. He absorbs each and every one of the special powers that the demons possess and has immediate access to them, increasing his fighting techniques exponentially.

Naraku grows more powerful by the day. At first, he runs away when faced with the threat of direct confrontation. Increasingly, he hardens himself to the prospect of fighting.

In battle, Naraku morphs into something gigantic, with a plethora of feelers emerging from the lower part of his body. His entire body is as strong as steel, and he exudes an extreme evil that, apart from protecting him like a force field, is able to repel any other force field close by. He is clearly InuYasha's greatest threat.

See Glossary
Naraku
Demon
InuYasha

See questions
41

InuYasha Key Chain

InuYasha fans are not going to want to miss out on yet another Movic tie-in with the movie Swords of an Honorable Ruler - this highly detailed key chain.

Although rather chunky, this double-figure key chain is a must-have for the serious collector.

Dangling from one chain, we have InuYasha from the waist up. His gray hair swirls around him as he is frozen in the act of unsheathing the deadly Tessaiga. Remarkably, a wry smile is depicted on his face, as if he's actually relishing the soon-to-come combat.

On the opposing chain, also linked to the same key-ring, is his half-brother Sesshomaru. As often, he looks undisturbed by the goings-on, simply staring straight ahead, his right hand supporting the Saimyosho hive he is shouldering.

Both figures can be removed so that you have a choice of who you want dangling from your front door key.

Movic
$6.00
© 2003 Takahashi Rumiko/Shogakkan/
Yomiuri TV/Sunrise/Shogakkan Production/
Toho/Yomiuri TV Enterprise

47 What kinds of destructive techniques does Naraku possess?

Naraku is particularly skilled at techniques that allow him to attack his opponents from a distance, inflicting damage on his opponents with his feeler-like tentacles.

See Glossary
Naraku

With one of these techniques, Naraku sucks the soul out of his opponent merely by touching it with one of his tentacles. Those that have been attacked in this manner become possessed by a darkness that brings sadness, fear and ambivalence into their hearts. That darkness is said to manifest itself as an apparition, and the afflicted opponent dies of despair.

Naraku's body is filled with poison and he is capable of inflicting great damage on his opponents by releasing it. This poison melts the very earth around Naraku, meaning no opponent can even get close to him.

He also makes frequent use of the Kugutsu, or puppet-fighting style, in order to allow him to avoid direct confrontations. With this technique, Naraku casts a spell on a clay doll, turning it into an image of himself that he then manipulates from afar.

As this alter ego has equal capabilities to Naraku, it is extremely strong. If beaten in battle, the image merely reverts to the clay it was made from, leaving Naraku unharmed.

We should not forget that Naraku has also managed to obtain a large number of the Shikon jewel's fragments, which he has reconstituted. This gives him the power to spawn other demons. He breaks off body parts of the demons he has absorbed in the past, and places them in jars to create new demons. These become his slaves after he casts the spell of fuko - "priestess insect sorcery" - on them

The spell comes from an old Chinese curse, originally used to bring creatures such as frogs, scorpions and spiders together in one place so that they would feed off each other. The creature that emerged from all this was known as a kodoku. A person eating this kodoku would be bestowed with the power to cast spells.

See Glossary
Shikon jewel

See questions
14

48 What kinds of demons has Naraku managed to produce?

Naraku has generated such demons as Goshinki, Kagura, Kanna, Juromaru and Kageromaru. They are all unique in appearance, but their looks are influenced by the individual demon Naraku has used to spawn them.

While they are all Naraku's slaves, they have wills of their own, and do not always carry out Naraku's orders to the letter. There is probably some poetic justice in the fact that although born of Naraku, these demons are demonic to the rotten core.

For example, Kagura, a female demon who can control the wind, has never fully accepted Naraku's control, and often reacts against his orders. But her life is in his hands, and she can be snuffed out at any moment if she refuses to obey.

See Glossary

Naraku
Demon
Goshinki
Kagura
Kanna
Juromaru
Kageromaru

See questions
41 46

49 What are the Saimyosho demons?

Saimyosho are the wasp-like demons that buzz around Naraku. Unlike the demons he has produced, the Saimyosho are totally enslaved to Naraku.

Saimyosho, which carry a potent poison in their bodies, were originally bred by Naraku in order to penetrate Miroku's black hole. If sucked into the hole, the Saimyosho would possibly contaminate Miroku and eventually kill him. Of course, this also means that Miroku cannot use his black hole as a weapon when Saimyosho are out and about.

Saimyosho are also capable of carrying fragments of the Shikon jewel, acting as spies to reconnoiter distant locations, and relaying information on everything they have seen and heard to Naraku.

See Glossary
Saimyosho
Demon
Naraku
Miroku
Kazana
Shikon jewel

See questions
14 22

Other InuYasha Inhabitants

InuYasha Profile 007
Name: Black Priestess Tsubaki

For a long time Tsubaki was a normal priestess, with similar spiritual powers to Kikyo. But when they fought over the Shikon jewel, Tsubaki - afraid of losing her looks - threw in her lot with the demons in exchange for eternal youth. Her art is to curse people to their deaths.

黒

巫

女 椿

Tsubaki was once a regular priestess, just like Kikyo. It is recorded that her spiritual powers were on a par with those of Kikyo. When Sango's father extracted the Shikon jewel from the body of a dead demon, he sought out a priestess to cleanse it of its evil, and in the end it was Kikyo who performed that role.

However, it was the teacher of Kikyo and Tsubaki who decided which one was more suitable for the task. Tsubaki was unhappy with the decision, and protested to her teacher. She could not accept she had not been consigned to the task, as her spiritual powers equaled those of Kikyo.

The reason she was not chosen was not because of her powers; it was because of what lay in her heart. It appears that she was concerned about growing old and losing her looks, and her teacher was worried that if he handed over the jewel to Tsubaki, she would use it to retain her youth.

⑤ee Glossary
Black Priestess (Tsubaki)
Kikyo
Sango's father
Shikon jewel
Demon

Out of resentment, Tsubaki - who had hoped to use the jewel precisely for that purpose - attempted to lay a curse on Kikyo using a snake. The curse was easily repelled by Kikyo, and rebounded onto Tsubaki, entering her body through her right eye, snake and all.

As a result, Tsubaki, who sought eternal youth and beauty, ends up with ugly snake-like scales around her eye. Her ugliness was too much for her to stomach, and she ends up selling her soul to the demons even while maintaining her sacred position as priestess.

Is it a good trade? You decide. In exchange for her soul she acquires eternal youth and the magical powers of the demons. As proof that she has sold out, from that day forth she dispenses with the standard white costume of a priestess, and instead adopts the color of evil - black. This explains why she is known as the Black Priestess.

See questions
30

Tsubaki sets the shikigami on Kagome, causing it to bite her. From this she manages to obtain some of Kagome's blood, which allows her to control the reincarnation of her rival. She attempts to have Kagome kill InuYasha, but her curses will not work on the girl, and bounce right back on her just as they did with Kikyo. Tsubaki also used the shikigami when she attempted to curse Kikyo some 50 years ago. The shikigami is not a demon. It was originally made from paper, but became a monster after being cursed. The paper was probably cut into the shape of a snake, with the curse added later. Shikigami is the generic name for monsters produced in this way. At one stage, two miko, who are junior to Tsubaki, team up as the red and white miko. Ignorant of the fact that Tsubaki has sold her soul to the demons, they challenge InuYasha to a fight on her behalf. They produce monsters using the shikigami magic, which they set upon InuYasha and his gang. But the girls' magic is underdeveloped, and the shikigami revert to paper.

See Glossary

Black Priestess
  (Tsubaki)
Shikigami
InuYasha
Kikyo
Miko

InuYasha Profile 008
Name: Koga

Koga is the young leader of the demon wolf pack. Relations within the pack are very strong, with each wolf looking out for the others. Koga and pack are on the trail of Naraku, their hatred whipped up after seeing many of their friends killed by him.

Koga can control the wolf pack at will. He is fleet of foot and can climb the steepest of rock faces. He pounces on his opponents, tearing them limb from limb with his sharp claws.

Koga has also fallen for Kagome, and considers InuYasha a rival. But Kagome doesn't even consider poor Koga a possibility, and his love goes nowhere.

52 Why can Koga run so fast?

Koga is a demon-wolf and is by far the fastest runner in the pack. But there is a secret to his speed. Koga has fragments of the Shikon jewel embedded in his legs. In other words, Koga is jewel-powered!

Koga also carries a sword, but seldom has need to use it, taking full advantage of his legs to engage in hand-to-hand (foot-to-hand?) fighting. He pounces on his opponents, tearing them apart with his sharp claws, which are unique to the demon-wolves.

As a wolf, Koga has honed his natural connection with all things wild. When he senses danger, his legs carry him to safety in no time, where he hides until danger has passed.

See Glossary
Koga
Wolf-Demons
Shikon jewel

See questions
14 15 16

InuYasha Note Pad

I doubt whether InuYasha ever attended school. However, if he did, he could of done worse than to practice his brushstrokes in this appealing note pad.

On the cover, we find the two half brothers. InuYasha's all hot and sweaty, as Tessaiga burns with energy. Sesshomaru, beside him, is more thoughtful, his hand on the hilt of the unsheathed Tenseiga. Behind them the full moon rises, silhouetting Koga leaping through the night sky.

On the back cover are six stills from the movie Swords of an Honorable Ruler, all of which depict the two half-brothers coming to blows. Inside, each of the 48 pages are emblazoned with the movie logo - Sesshomaru and InuYasha in combat framed in a crescent moon and Miroku's staff.

Altogether, it's an impressive collectible, and surely makes mincemeat out of the usually dull note pads that most students get stuck with.

Movic
$3.00
18 cm x 25 cm
© 2003 Takahashi Rumiko/Shogakkan/
Yomiuri TV/Sunrise/Shogakkan
Production/Toho/Yomiuri TV Enterprise

53 What is it between Kagome and Koga?

Koga believes in looking out for the other guy, and is trusted by the pack as a straight shooter. But there is a flipside to his character: he is impetuous to the point where he'll attack an opponent no matter how strong it may be.

Although we can praise him for being uncomplicated, he is not good at thinking things through.

This is what happens when he meets Kagome: he falls for her immediately. It is not a case of what it is about her that he likes, or what kind of person she is - he just wants her as his woman. All else is irrelevant.

Koga and InuYasha of course become rivals in love. Although the two share the same aim, that of defeating Naraku, their love-rivalry prevents Koga from following in the tracks of Miroku and Sango and joining the InuYasha gang. But Koga is Koga, straight as an arrow, and we know he will help InuYasha if he's ever in real need.

See Glossary
Koga
InuYasha
Naraku
Miroku
Sango

123

InuYasha Profile 009
Name: Kaede

Kaede is the younger sister of Kikyo, and follows in her footsteps as a priestess. She is far from equal to her elder sister when it comes to spiritual powers, but still has considerable powers of her own. These include the rosary beads that she places around InuYasha's neck. She can also conjure up a force field, and she possesses the ability to sense evil. It is Kaede who orders InuYasha and Kagome to search out the scattered shards of the Shikon jewel.

Kaede is a serving miko, which explains her not be married. Miko remain single so they can give themselves fully to the gods. Marrying would cause the gods to be jealous, resulting in the weakening of the miko's spiritual powers.

Japanese gods are not the invisible, spiritually aloof entities seen in western religions. They can be extremely earthy creatures that experience the same mundane emotions as human beings, such as anger, jealousy and lust. There is no attempt to worship them as paragons of absolute or transcendental good.

However, it is best to treat them with respect and reverence, as the anger of the gods is believed to manifest itself in the form of typhoons and natural disasters. Alternatively, when the gods are happy, they reward their subjects with bumper harvests.

Not all natural disasters can be attributed to the gods raining down retribution on the wicked - sometimes they just feel like having a bit of fun.

See Glossary
Kaede
Miko

InuYasha Writing Board

Japanese kids are a diligent lot. When they're not at school, or juku (cram school), you can find them commandeering the tables at the local fast food outlet, with their school books uncracked, their pens uncased, and their requisite one soda long drunk.

The writing board, therefore, is an essential piece of their armory, allowing them to swat through the night on the most roughest or stickiest of surfaces.

Enter InuYasha. On the front of this attractive writing board, we find InuYasha with Tessaiga in hand probably about to swipe his half-brother, Sesshomaru, whose good looks are reflected in the blade. In the background, but equally prepared to battle

against evil are the gang - Miroku, Sango and Kagome.

The reverse side is less colorful, but features a host of characters, including the odd-looking Jaken and the retainer flea, Myoga.

In fact, the whole thing is so appealing, it's almost a pity to have to cover it up with tomorrow's homework.

Movic
$2.00   18 cm x 25.5 cm

55 What are Kaede's powers as a miko?

Kaede's power is expressed in a number of ways. She cooperates with Miroku to create a force field around the hall covering Kikyo's grave when Urasue comes close to stealing the dead body. But this is not a powerful field, and will disintegrate if Kaede moves or is simply distracted.

Like Kikyo and Kagome, when Kaede fights the demons she does so with a bow and arrow. Although powerful, the charmed arrows she lets loose cannot be compared to those of her elder sister - Kikyo - and Kikyo's incarnation - Kagome.

When the pressure is on, her powers cannot compete with those of Kikyo. However, her age and experience combine to make her a capable and reliable advisor to InuYasha and his gang.

See Glossary

Kaede
Miroku
Kikyo
Urasue
InuYasha
Demon

See questions
17 32

InuYasha Profile 010
Name: Totosai

Totosai is a blacksmith who has made sword-smithing his life's work. It is Totosai who crafts the renowned swords Tessaiga and Tenseiga from the fangs of Sesshomaru and InuYasha's father.

He appears out of nowhere on the back of a three-eyed ox, and at first seems something of an opportunist. This, however, probably reflects the flexibility of his personality. After having done business with the demons for many years, he has learned to adapt to their ever-changing moods.

The extent of Totosai's abilities as a demon is to emit flames from his mouth. He has also been known to jump with an agility seldom seen in one so old, and catch the Tessaiga swung by InuYasha using only a tanned animal skin. But, as demonic powers go, they don't amount to much.

There are probably a large number of demons like Totosai who, because they are not so strong, need to carry arms. This is where Totosai excels - as a sword smith he is unbeatable. Indeed, we can probably make a case for Totosai being ahead of his time in realizing the need for weaponry to offset a lack of strength.

As well as a respected sword smith, Totosai has a keen sense for business, and he treats all demons equally, showing no particular favor for InuYasha. He appears to have had a great respect for InuYasha's father, who was indeed a great demon, and based on this has high hopes for InuYasha.

Like other older characters in the series,

See Glossary
Totosai
Demon
Tessaiga
InuYasha

such as Kaede and Myogajii, his age and experience make him a worthy advisor for InuYasha. We should also keep in mind that scientific knowledge was rare at the time, and knowledge passed down from old to young was a valuable source of information.

See Glossary
Kaede
Myogajii

See questions
3 9 37

The Demons of InuYasha

Gatenmaru (Demon Moth)

Gatenmaru is the demon of a moth that has morphed into human form and taken over the body of a bandit. His specialty is the use of a poisonous powder, which he uses on InuYasha and Miroku when they realize what he is.

He immobilizes InuYasha with a thick mucus, causing him to release Tessaiga. Gatenmaru intends to wrap InuYasha up in a poisonous cocoon that will melt him once encased, but at the last moment Miroku sets up a force field with his trusty staff - Shakujo.

InuYasha is overcome by the poison, and only his heart is left beating. But an angry red glow begins to burn within his eyes as he calls on his demon powers. Theses powers rise within him, and he bursts out of the cocoon with fangs exposed and ready for the kill.

Gatenmaru also reverts to his demon origins and blasts InuYasha with all the poisonous powder he has. He then tries netting him with the threads of the poisonous cocoon, but the demon in InuYasha makes him totally immune to the attacks, and he slashes the bothersome moth in two with his claws.

Gokurakucho

Demon birds with human-like upper bodies and bird-like torsos, and that chew with mouths in the center of their bodies. The leaders of the tribe are twin brothers cojoined with a gigantic body. Their great powers stem from their possessing a shard of the Shikon jewel.

Goshinki

Goshinki is the third demon spawned by Naraku. He is able to read people's minds, which comes in handy as a fighting technique because he can tell what his opponents are going to do next.

His fangs are strong enough to smash the legendarily resilient Tessaiga, but he is eventually ripped limb from limb by InuYasha.

It is ironic that Goshinki's fangs are forged into the Tokijin by the renegade sword smith Kaijinbo at the request of Sesshomaru.

Hiten and Manten (The Thunder Brothers)

Two brothers; the elder is adept at fighting with thunder, and the younger fights with heat. They are responsible for the death of Shippo's father, and become the sworn enemy of Shippo.

The two brothers are not at all alike. The demonic power of the elder brother, Hiten, is heightened after he inserts a shard of the Shikon jewel into his forehead. He becomes a cruel and excitable killer.

The younger brother, Manten, has the looks of a balding monster, of which he has developed quite a complex. It was a hama no ya arrow let loose by Kagome that shaved off most of his hair, sending Manten into a rage. He releases a thunderbolt at Kagome, who manages to escape by the skin of her teeth, but is knocked out by the shock wave.

Manten is enthralled with Kagome, and instead of killing her, picks her up, tucks her under his arm and carries her off. He intends to make his own hair tonic by boiling down her body.

Kagome comes to in the brothers' castle, and is shocked when she learns of Manten's sinister plans for her. Hiten arrives carrying another girl, and Kagome is relieved for a moment as Hiten looks almost human. But she soon changes her mind when she sees him incinerate the young girl without a second thought.

Kagome's wits are now working overtime, and after finding out that the brothers are also after the shards of the Shikon jewel, she manages to come up with a plausible reason for them to go charging off after InuYasha.

InuYasha deflects Hiten's thunder spear and blade with Tessaiga, but it is a tough fight, and InuYasha has a hard time of it, if only because he cannot stop thinking about Kagome. He eventually manages to kill Manten. In his despair, Hiten chooses to eat the dead flesh of Manten, which increases his own powers. He attacks InuYasha, but also falls to Tessaiga.

Hyoneko Shitenno (Four Kings of the Leopard-Cat Tribe)

Shunran, Karan, Shuran and Toran are the four kings of the Hyoneko tribe that came out of the west 50 years ago to settle the score with Sesshomaru. Their names are taken from those of the four seasons, and roughly translate into Spring Storm, Summer Storm, Autumn Storm and Winter Storm.

Karan, one of the four kings, turns up in Kaede's village while InuYasha is in the present day meeting with Kagome. Karan's aim is to capture Kagome and the shards of the Shikon jewel, but he immediately leaves once he hears she is not there.

Later, Toran appears before Sesshomaru to tell him that he will be waiting at the castle to settle the 50-year-old feud. Sesshomaru takes Jaken with him and sets off for the castle.

Shunran, Karan and Shuran appear before InuYasha, who knows nothing of this fight as he has been sealed up in the sacred tree for 50 years. InuYasha moves to withdraw Tessaiga from its sheath, but is attacked by a ball of fire.

InuYasha somehow manages to jump out of the way, only to see that Karan is coated in flame. Shuran is taking on Miroku and Sango, Shunran lets drop a petal, and Kagome, who has been watching from the safety, passes out. The three kings make off with Kagome and the shards of the jewel. They shout that if InuYasha wants to see Kagome alive again then he and his friends should come to the castle...then disappear.

InuYasha runs into Koga on his way to the castle while following the scent left by the feline Hyoneko kings. When Koga hears Kagome has been taken, he sets off for the castle with InuYasha. InuYasha then breaks through the force field into a hidden village, and the four kings come out in a counter-attack.

Things get more confusing when Sesshomaru appears and tells InuYasha not to get involved in his long-standing fight with the Hyoneko. Sesshomaru then takes off for the castle alone.

InuYasha doesn't have a clue what's going on, that is until Myogajii relates to him how his father had won a great battle over the Hyoneko tribe in the west 50 years before. But though weakened, the spirit of the Hyoneko survived, and they swore vengeance on the victor's entire family with a blood-curdling curse.

Karan attacks at just that moment, releasing innumerable balls of fire that set the entire area aflame. Miroku and Sango somehow manage to break through the raging fires, but are caught up in a surprise attack by Shuran.

Koga meets up with Okaminoboshi in the hidden village while looking for Kagome. There, he too hears for the first time of the battle 50 years before. Okaminoboshi relates how he was no use to Sesshomaru, crumbling in the face of the attack and becoming deadweight for the man he was supposed to be helping.

InuYasha, Koga and Sesshomaru reach the castle of the Hyoneko, but have a hard time of it in the fight against the four kings. They eventually manage to repel them and enter the castle to save Kagome. But the supreme general of the Hyoneko tribe - Odatesama - kills three of the four kings and comes back to life.

Jinenji

Jinenji is a demi-demon like InuYasha. Huge in size, but warm of heart, he lives with his mother on the edge of the village. There they make a living by cultivating medicinal herbs.

Jinenji is often bullied by the villagers because of his appearance. Although he never retaliates, the villagers accuse Jinenji of attacking the locals girls. They call in InuYasha and the demon exterminators.

InuYasha senses no blood on Jinenji hands and, reasoning he cannot be the one responsible for the outrages, he leaves. As he does, he comes across the villagers gathering together weapons for an assault on Jinenji, and determines to find the true culprit and vindicate Jinenji.

In the meantime, Kagome pleads with the villagers not to attack Jinenji before InuYasha returns, and stays close to him, working alongside him in the fields. With Kagome, Jinenji learns true peace and begins to fall in love with her.

InuYasha attacks the lair of a demon hidden in the dark forest, but it is empty and has not been used for some time. Still, from the shell of an egg that he finds there, he realizes that the demon has taken her newly-hatched human-eating young to the village to attack the villagers. The villagers break their promise to Jinenji and attempt to kill him. The man-eating demon appears and Jinenji uses all his strength to protect Kagome.

The villagers finally realize that Jinenji is a kindred soul.

Juromaru and Kageromaru (Double Trouble!)

The fourth and fifth creations of Naraku, Juromaru and Kageromaru are the original evil twins, although one is inside the other like Russian dolls.

Juromaru's chiseled, expressionless doll-like face hides the cruelty that enables him to kill everything that passes before his eyes. But it is Kageromaru, curled up like a parasite inside Juromaru, who controls him. Juromaru listens to nobody but Kageromaru, and will attempt to kill anyone - even Naraku - on his orders.

When first spawned, they slice off Naraku's head and eat two of his palace guards. That explains why Naraku keeps Juromaru gagged and in manacles to bottle up Kageromaru.

Kageromaru is frighteningly intelligent and fast, and has

arms like scythes. The evil twins specialty is sneaking up on their enemies and ripping them apart with their sharp fangs.

Kagura
(Music and Dance to Please the Gods)

Kagura is one of the demons spawned by Naraku.

Kagura is of female form, and is extremely intelligent. She calls herself the personification of the wind, and can control the wind with a fan she always carries with her. As she is capable of ruling every breeze she produces by wafting the fan, it is also possible for her to surround herself with her demonic powers.

She is also able to increase the size of the feather she uses as a hair decoration, and fly off on a breeze she has created for herself.

Many of her fighting techniques are also based on this close association with the wind. These include Fujin no Mai - Dance of the Wind-Blade - by which a sharp wave of the fan produces wind-blades which strike her opponents. Another is Ryuja no Mai - Dance of the Serpent - where she revolves her fan in a cyclical pattern, producing a gigantic serpent-like twister.

She can also manipulate the bodies of the dead, as in Dance of the Corpses. As she can manipulate any number dead bodies in sequence, this can be used to great effect.

It soon becomes clear that Kagura wants to live as freely as the wind, and to her Naraku becomes an obstacle. She aggressively seeks out allies to help her overthrow the old demon, betraying him at every turn.

But Naraku has taken physical control of her heart, and she

would die if he decided to crush it. She has no option but to do as he says, and proof of a enslavement is in the spider's mark that she carries on her back.

Kaijinbo

Sword smith Kaijinbo produces nothing but evil swords. He was originally a pupil and apprentice of Totosai - who forged InuYasha's Tessaiga and Sesshomaru's Tenseiga - but was cast out by the master after he realized Kaijinbo was testing his swords on live human beings.

When Sesshomaru hears that Goshinki has bitten the all-powerful Tessaiga in two, he orders Kaijinbo to make the ultimate evil sword using the fangs of Naraku's third creation. This is Tokijin.

Kaijinbo is only too pleased to comply with the request - if only to get his own back on Totosai. But the sword Tokijin that Kaijinbo forges is so steeped in evil that it causes Kaijinbo himself go off the rails. He seeks out InuYasha, and it is a close fight until the reformed Tessaiga comes into its own and cuts Kaijinbo down.

Kanna (The Godless One)

Although Kanna appears as a young girl, she is the first demon that Naraku creates from himself. She is capable of a multitude of techniques using a mirror that Naraku has given her, but gives off no demonic force herself. This is an important factor however, as it means she can easily enter sacred places or the force field of other demons without being detected..

Kanna has no physical forms of attack, and is underdeveloped physically when compared to other creatures spawned by Naraku. She shows no emotion, and merely follows Naraku's orders. When we consider that she is Naraku's firstborn, it makes sense that she is closer to Naraku than a free-spirited demon like Kagura, and is therefore trusted by him.

Her powers are clairvoyant-like - she can see the goings-on of any particular place through her mirror. She can also suck in the soul of anybody whose reflection appears in the mirror, and then control them at will. Attacks by others also rebound if caught in the mirror. Because Kanna gives off no demonic force, she is also capable sneaking up close to her opponents and using her mirror on them.

Kotatsu (Hell's Painter)

The painter Kotatsu has run away from Kyoto. He is not a demon, but has somehow obtained the power to bring to life the pictures that he paints with sumi - Indian ink - after a shard of the Shikon jewel is mixed into his ink.

He comes across a beautiful princess, and attempts to have an ogre he has drawn bring her to him. He eagerly awaits her arrival, but when she does appear, she is being followed by the ladies man, Miroku.

Kotatsu begins to tell them his story. He painted scenes from hell, and traveled to battlefields, painting the corpses he found there. By chance, he came across a fragment of the jewel, melted it and mixed it into his ink. The demon he painted suddenly came to life.

He then discovers that a more powerful reaction can be obtained by mixing living liver and blood with his ink, and has had to escape from Kyoto after killing too many people to keep his powers alive. He then confesses that he has been painting the princess every night in order to one day have her as his own.

Miroku demands he hand over the shard of the jewel, but Kotatsu calls to life a hoard of demons from a picture he has painted and makes them attack Miroku. InuYasha appears with a clothes peg on his nose to fend off the smell, but the stench from so many demons is overwhelming and InuYasha faints.

Miroku opens the black hole in his hand, sucking in the hoard of demons. This leaves him exhausted by the overwhelming evil around him. Kotatsu chooses this moment to jump on a three-headed serpent and escapes by flying off into the sky.

InuYasha comes to and gives chase. Miroku shouts after him that Kotatsu is not a demon, but human, so InuYasha must be careful not to kill him. But InuYasha does not hear.

Mukadejoro (Mistress Centipede)

A demon whose lower body is a centipede, and whose upper body resembles a woman. Mukadejoro suddenly appears from the well at the Higurashi Shrine and attacks Kagome, causing her to fall into the well and enter the time warp back to the Era of Warring States.

Mukadejoro also enters the time warp, biting into the Shikon jewel, which was embedded in Kagome's side, and swallowing it. This causes Mukadejoro to morph into a gigantic and evil being.

Mukadejoro attacks not only Kagome, but also InuYasha, who is still sealed up in the sacred tree. The centipede is eventually killed by InuYasha after he has been released from his spell by Kagome.

Mukadejoro has no other features or powers to comment on. Appearing in the first episode as she does, we can only imagine that her role is to help introduce and emphasize the powers of the jewel, along with Kagome's spiritual powers.

Muso (Peerless)

We know that Naraku, a combination of different demons, can spawn demons to help him in his quest for the jewel. There are cases, however, when he also discards bodily parts that he believes are holding him back.

Muso is born from one such lump of discarded flesh. But the flesh also carries the spider's mark, a link to Onigumo, Naraku's original human form.

Born faceless and without memory, the entity kills a group of soldiers that first discover him in a pile of human offal. By doing this, he is hoping to find an adequate face, and tries each of the dead faces on one by one. But he is hard to please, and it is not until he kills the beautiful Buddhist monk Muso that he finds a face to suit his pride.

He steals the monk's name as well, and continues on his killing ways until he runs into InuYasha and his gang in a village close to where Kaede lives.

Muso seems to have a vague memory associated with Kagome, and tries to capture her, but is torn limb from limb by the

Kaze no Kizu released by InuYasha. His body clearly has recuperative powers, and quickly reforms itself. Muso finds himself making his way to the cave that Onigumo hid in 50 years before.

Here he meets up with Kagome once again, and Onigumo's memories begin to flood Muso's mind. He is chopped to pieces yet again by InuYasha, but manages to pick himself up and piece himself back together again no matter how many times this happens. InuYasha is rapidly running out of ideas on how to get rid of him.

InuYasha notices that the spider mark on Muso's back contains a heart, and directs the Kaze no Kizu at this vital point. However, Kagura suddenly appears, sending the Kaze no Kizu off course. To make things worse, Muso himself is suddenly carried off by the Saimyosho, forcing InuYasha to give chase.

Naraku then appears before Muso and tries to reabsorb him, but Muso has recovered all of Onigumo's mem ories and has grown to hate Naraku for what he did to Kikyo.

Just as Muso is trying to flee from Naraku, InuYasha appears, setting the stage for a three-way face off.

Naraku's tentacles attack InuYasha in the form of a spear, which InuYasha repels with Kaze no Kizu, but in terms of strength the two are equally matched. Muso pierces Naraku with his own tentacles. The Evil One not only manages to stand firm, but also retraces the course of the attacking tentacle and sucks Muso back into his own body, finally reabsorbing him.

Nikutsugino Men
(The Flesh-Eating Mask)

This is the name of a wooden Noh mask that has been in the posses-sion of the Higurashi family since the warring states period.

The mask was carved from the trunk of an ancient cinna-mon tree that had a shard of the Shikon jewel embedded in it. The story is that once the mask is placed on someone's face, it cannot be removed until the victim dies.

Kagome is forced to return to the present day from the Era of Warring States to sit her high school entrance exams. While she is at school taking the test, there is a fire in the warehouse at Higurashi Shrine.

Kagome's grandfather sees smoke billowing from the doors of the warehouse, and approaches it to put out the fire. But the fire has burnt the seal that keeps the spell of the Noh mask under con-trol, and the mask starts to run amok, attacking Kagome's grandfa-ther.

He attempts to fight off the Noh mask with a sacred tag, but is knocked out by a burning beam that falls from the roof of the warehouse.

Kagome sees the fire trucks in front of the shrine when she returns from school and rushes to her mother. The fire is already under control, but the Noh mask has been unwittingly swept up by one of the fireman, and is now attacking a fire truck. The Noh mask gets bigger and bigger as it sucks more victims into its vortex.

Kagome and her younger brother, Sota, are left at home after her mother goes to the hospital to be with Kagome's grandfa-ther. It is not long before she realizes that the events of the day have been caused by a shard of the jewel that has been brought back from the past.

The Flesh-Eating Mask chooses this moment to attack, aiming to get the jewel shard. Kagome uses herself as a lure, allowing Sota to escape and call InuYasha from the well. Sota jumps into the well, but he cannot go through the time warp. InuYasha, however, suddenly appears from nowhere.

InuYasha throws Sota onto his back and quickly follows the scent of blood to track down Kagome. Meanwhile, Kagome is hiding out on a construction site. She has no place to go, so starts to climb the half-constructed building, but the Noh mask soon catches up with her.

InuYasha appears in the nick of time, slicing up the meaty face of the mask. But the body of the mask continues to move. The mask is believed to be indestructible, even against fire, and anyone who attempts to destroy it will meet with death. But Kagome has heard that the forehead of the mask - in which the shard is embedded - is its weak spot, and InuYasha swings his sword at the spot, destroying the mask.

Nise-Suijin (False Water God)

The false Water God is actually a sprite or genie in the form of a dragon that serves the true Water God. The true god is a small female entity. She is tricked and held prisoner, while the false Water God seizes her sacred treasure - the Amakoi Halberd - and demands the villagers surrender their children as sacrifices.

InuYasha and gang are called upon to exterminate the false Water God and save the child of a servant who has been sent to be sacrificed as a substitute for one of the lord's children. They attack the Water God's shrine in the middle of the lake, but are sent to the bottom of the lake by a spell emanating from the divine power of the Amakoi Halberd.

Kagome comes to her wits and fires a hama no ya arrow. It splinters one of Water God's arms, giving InuYasha just enough time to escape the shrine. He is helped in his efforts by the goldfish that serve the true Water God. He is told the true Water God is imprisoned in a rock, and that a dragon spirit has stolen the sacred treasure and assumed her identity.

InuYasha saves the true Water God, and the false Water God is sent to the bottom of the sea in a whirlpool whipped up by the Amakoi Halberd.

Okami Noboshi

Known as the Wolf of Hell, he has a flat face and round eyes. He is, in fact, a warm-hearted demon who would not normally hurt anyone, but he runs amok and attacks InuYasha after Naraku implants in him a shard of the Shikon jewel. InuYasha is hard put to defend himself after Okami Noboshi spews a three-eyed wolf from his mouth. But once the shard is removed from his forehead, Noboshi returns to his normal easy-going self. He exits the story with a smile on his face.

Oni no Kubi Shiro no Oni

The long name of a demon whose head was buried under a castle to ward off evil spirits many years before.

InuYasha and his gang help an old woman exorcist, who is being attacked after failing to exterminate a pack of weasel demons. She asks them to exterminate the demon in the Demon's Head Castle.

The demon's head appears before InuYasha and friends exuding pure evil, and easily repels any attack the gang can mount. But Miroku realizes they are fighting an apparition, and hurls two sacred scrolls at it. It disappears before their very eyes, and the evil dissolves.

The demon is actually the princess of the castle, who sets about seducing Miroku. Sango can see what is happening and is about to unleash her weapon - Hiraikotsu - but instead she is frozen where she stands.

Just as the demon-princess looks set to eat Miroku raw, the old woman appears. The demon-princess tries to cast an evil spell on the old woman, but it has no effect. Miroku tells the old woman to scatter purifying ash-salt on the demon-princess while he creates a seal, which he instills with his sacred powers. These powers cause the ash to explode, and the demon-princess escapes with nothing but her head.

Kagome discovers the rem ains of the real princess in the sleeping chamber of the lord of the castle, but is attacked through the mosquito net by the head of the demon-princess. The remains of the real princess start to glow and mysterious balls of Buddhist power kaleidoscope off the princess into the mouth of the demon-princess. It turns out that the demon had been storing this mysteri-ous power in the remains of the princess.

The demon-princess is now fully powered, and when she finds out that Kagome is carrying a shard of the Shikon jewel, she attacks. Kagome whips some medicinal alcohol out of a first-aid box and throws it in demon-princess' face. Shippo also lets loose his fox-fire on her and they both try to escape while the demon-princess is in flames.

But the demon-princess uses her powers to bring down the roof, trapping Kagome and Shippo, who only manage to escape at the last moment.

Ryukotsusei (Essence of the Dragon)

Ryukotsusei is the demon of a gigantic dragon that InuYasha's father once battled with and eventually entombed. The dragon has an extra face carved in its forehead like a vortex, issues scorching flames from its mouth, has a hide stronger than steel, and refuses to die - even when pierced through the heart.

Totosai has repaired Tessaiga using one of InuYasha's own fangs, but the sword becomes too heavy for InuYasha to swing. Totosai tells the demi-demon that it is because InuYasha's fangs are not as strong as those of his father. InuYasha is in a bind, because if he lets go of Tessaiga he reverts to his demon roots, which sends him out of control.

Totosai tells InuYasha the only way to make the sword lighter is to kill Ryukotsusei and surpass the exploits of his illustrious father.

InuYasha is against killing the dragon while it remains entombed. This moral problem is solved when the dragon is freed by Naraku. Now he can fight one on one.

The dragon is much more nimble than its size suggests. It attacks InuYasha, who brings down Tessaiga with all his might on the dragon's claws as they threaten to rip him apart. But the sword is too weighty and registers no impact.

But InuYasha manages to infuse his trusty weapon with his fighting spirit, and the sword becomes lighter and lighter, allowing InuYasha to swing it with greater ease. InuYasha lunges at the dragon and pierces its heart with the Tessaiga. This sets off Kaze no Kizu, which envelopes them both, It does prove, however, that InuYasha can now set off the technique at will.

But the dragon is unscathed, and InuYasha is forced to rapidly master the Bakuryuha to overcome it. In the instant he disposes of Ryukotsusei, InuYasha surpasses the exploits of his father.

Sakasagami yoma Yura (Yura of the Demon Hair)

Yura must be the sexiest demon there is in the InuYasha series! She can control her hair at will, tying down her opponents so they cannot move, and using it to make the bodies of the dead dance like marionettes.

She launches an attack on InuYasha, because she has decided he is in the way of her own search for the shards of the Shikon jewel.

Her other weapons include a sword named Koro, and Onibukushi (Demon Firecombs). Yura is in fact a demonized hairbrush, with her spirit sealed up inside the comb.

As a result, her human form can be killed many times over, but she keeps coming back to life until the brush itself is destroyed. Only Kagome can do this, as she is the only one who can see Yura's hair, and traces it back to its roots in the comb, which she successfully destroys.

Shibugarasu (Corpse Dancing Crow)

Shibugarasu originally resembles a normal crow - but with three eyes! He is relatively small, and his fighting powers are limited. However, when he swallows the Shikon jewel, he morphs into a gigantic bird of prey, and becomes increasingly fierce.

Shibugarasu also attains phoenix-like qualities thanks to the jewel. This allows him to reconstitute himself and rise from the dead, even if he is torn limb from limb and his body scattered throug hout the land. He also has the annoying ability to be able to burrow into the corpses of the dead, so that he can control them to attack other human beings.

It is because Shibugarasu swallows the jewel and attempts to fly off that Kagome is forced to shoot her hama no ya, not only downing Shibugarasu, but also causing the jewel to shatter. This is what sets InuYasha and his gang off on their journey to recover the shards of the jewel.

Shiori

Shiori is demi-demon, born of Tsukuyomaru - a bat-demon - and a human mother. She has the power to establish and control force fields, an ability in which she surpasses even her father, who died in somewhat my sterious circumstances while she was still a baby.

Shiori's grandfather is Taibokumaru, an elder of the bat tribe. He promises not to attack the village where Shiori resides if he is given his grandchild. The villagers agree, but once Taibokumaru has taken charge of Shiori, he immediately breaks his promise and attacks.

InuYasha and gang are approaching this same village after having been told by Totosai that in order to break down Naraku's powerful force field, it is necessary to kill the demon that has created the force field and bathe the blade of Tessaiga in its blood. On approaching the village from the west, InuYasha and gang run into Shizu, a young woman who has been treated badly by the villagers. She explains to InuYasha what is going on. It turns out she is Shiori's mother. The villagers have turned on her to avenge the attack of the bat tribe. InuYasha understands then that he must not only kill a demi-demon like himself, but a little girl no less.

InuYasha has Shizu lead him and his friends to the cave where Taibokumaru is holed up. They are taken to a glimmering cave protected by a force field put in place by none other than Shiori herself.

In the ensuing fight, Shiori learns that it was Taibokumaru who killed her father and pushes him outside the force field. He releases a demon sound wave at the young girl, but is blasted by a full power Bakuryuha which InuYasha releases.

Tatari-Mokke

Tatari-Mokke is a demon given life by the souls of young children. Originally a demon that looked after the spirits of deceased children until they could attain Buddha-hood, Tatari-Mokke also guides souls likely to bring forth plagues and disasters into the present world to hell.

Kagome returns from the Era of Warring States for the first

time in a week, and accompanies her younger brother Sota to the hospital where he is visiting his sick friend, Satoru, who has been in a coma since a fire broke out some six months before.

Kagome sees a girl in hospital who she saw playing in the park the previous day. Kagome realizes that this is the spirit of Mayu, Satoru's elder sister, who was killed in the same fire. Mayu is looking for a chance to take Sota's life out of a deep-seated grudge.

When the fire broke out, Mayu's and Satoru's mother did everything to save Satoru, not realizing that Mayu was also trapped in the fire. Mayu misinterprets what has happened and returns as a vengeful spirit, aiming to take revenge on Satoru.

Kagome sees Tatari-Mokke hovering over the soul of Mayu, but the look of sadness in Mayu's eyes makes Kagome feel she has to do something to help the unfortunate girl. She talks to Mayu about what happened during the fire, and gets her to understand that it was not the fault of her mother or her brother.

By doing this, Kagome prevents Tatari-Mokke from guiding the soul of Mayu down to hell, and succeeds in pointing her on her way to heaven.

Tokajin (Peach Man)

Tokajin is the demonized form of a man who ate his master so as to assume his powers and achieve immortality.

Tokajin turns the villagers into human-faced fruit. Their heads sprout from a tree like fruit, which he then eats as an elixir. The unfortunate fruit tell their story to InuYasha, who in turn decides to help them.

InuYasha attempts to cut down the tree, which grows on

the side of a cliff, but is confronted by Tokajin. InuYasha flashes Tessaiga, but his attack is repelled. Tokajin then sucks the demi-demon into a gourd he carries with him. It is the night of the full moon, and InuYasha has temporarily lost his powers.

Kagome, Miroku and Shippo grow concerned, and attempt to follow InuYasha up the face of the cliff. However, they become trapped in Tokajin's miniature garden, where he keeps his prey. Kagome tries to escape, but instead is carried off by Tokajin. Miroku and Shippo eventually escape and go in search of InuYasha.

Kagome is taken to a room where InuYasha is bound up with thorny vines. He tries to tear these up in anger when he sees her, but to no avail. Meanwhile, Miroku is watching from afar, and unleashes his black hole, which sucks up the thorns and brings down the roof.

Tokajin is buried alive, and Miroku, Shippo and the injured InuYasha use this opportunity to rescue Kagome. InuYasha has lost too much blood and collapses in a comatose state.

Kagome discovers a flower with the face of the original master next to the tree of human fruit.

According to the master, he has been changed into a flower so Tokajin can get him to reveal how to make the elixir of life.

Tokajin returns, crashing in on this scene, and fights it out with InuYasha, who can do little to deter him in his injured state. The old master changes into a bow and arrow in an attempt to atone for his mistake, allowing Kagome to fire an arrow at his ex-pupil. The brightly burning arrow cuts through Tokajin, dislodging a shard of the Shikon jewel. Tokajin lunges desperately at Kagome, but InuYasha comes between them. The two fall over the edge of the cliff.

Tsukumo no Gama (The Demon Toad)

Tsukumo no Gama is a demon that takes the form of a 300-year-old toad, and gains his demonic powers from sealing the bodies of kidnapped young maidens in toad-spawn and eating them after they have ripened.

During their quest to recover and reform the Shikon jewel, InuYasha, Kagome and Myogajii run across the young Samurai of the Takeda clan - Nobunaga Amari.

Although Amari comes across as a bit dumb, he has an important mission. He has come to confirm reports that the lord of the castle, who Princess Tsuyu of the Takeda clan has married, has gone insane. InuYasha and the gang also hear that this young lord has fallen prey to demons, and have come to exterminate them.

Amari and the InuYasha gang sneak into the castle, where everyone is sleeping under a demonic spell. Amari eventually finds Princess Tsuyu, only to come face to face with the heavily bandaged lord of the castle. One fell swoop of InuYasha's claws cut the bandages away to reveal the face of a toad! The face of Tsukumono no Gama.

He breathes a vaporous poison from his mouth that throws InuYasha to the floor seizing his throat. The toad then seizes Princess Tsuyu and make his getaway. Amari draws his sword to stop the toad, but is badly injured for his troubles.

The room Tsukumono no Gama escapes into is awash in toad spawn containing the young girls of the village - almost like a scene from Alien. InuYasha wades in with Tessaiga drawn, and attacks. But Tsukumono no Gama quickly heals his wounds by eating the young women as they hatch from the spawn.

Amari attempts to save Princess Tsuyu from the spawn, but is set upon by the toad. InuYasha thwacks the toad with the blunt edge of Tessaiga, allowing the heart of the young lord to emerge while Tsukumono no Gama is still reeling from the blow.

The young lord realizes that he will soon be totally consumed by the demon, and pleads with Amari to kill him and Princess Tsuyu together. Amari cannot do this, and attempts to defend the young lord.

Kagome has heard from Myogajii that Tsukumono no Gama cannot stand heat, so she sprays her hair spray into the flame of a lamp that Hiyoshimaru - Amari's monkey - has brought with him. This explodes right into the face of Tsukumono no Gama, allowing the lord of the castle to escape while the odious toad is disposed of with a single stroke of InuYasha's Tessaiga.

Urasue (Divination)

Urasue is the demon of an old woman - a Grim Reaperess - who carries a sickle. She uses the sickle to dig up the bones of the dead, bring them back to life, and control them at her will.

She opens up the grave of Kikyo, stealing her dead body and some of the earth around it, and revives the miko in order to obtain the fragments of the Shikon jewel. But the body of Kikyo is a mere shell, with no soul remaining. Urasue realizes that the soul has already been reincarnated in a different body.

When she discovers that Kikyo's soul resides in the body of Kagome, Urasue kidnaps the girl, and tries to separate Kikyo's soul from Kagome's body. But the soul is protected by a powerful force field.

InuYasha arrives at that moment, and calls out Kikyo's name without realizing what he is doing. Kikyo's soul reacts to the call by breaking through the force field, leaving the body of Kagome, and enters her own revitalized body.

Urasue then attempts to use Kikyo to kill InuYasha, but Kikyo still maintains powerful spiritual powers, and not only does she avoid falling under the control of the cunning Urasue, but manages to blast her to bits.

Kikyo fires a hama no ya arrow at InuYasha, who is defenseless. But just as the arrow is about to hit its target, Kagome awakens, leading to the collapse in Kikyo. Like someone shot with a gun, her knees buckle under her. Bright shining balls of light leave Kikyo's body and enter Kagome. But the desire for vengeance burns brightly in the body of Kikyo. As a result, she ends up remaining on this earth as a vengeful spirit.

InuYasha Hand Towel

In the sticky heat of the Japanese summer, every man, woman and child seems to be continually dabbing their sweaty foreheads with a small hand towel. It is as much a part of summer here as is the stamina-building dish of eel and the chilled glass of beer.

Kagome would be one such towel-carrier, and it is probably with her in mind that Movic released the InuYasha - The Movie hand towel.

In simple red and black, the towel depicts the two half-brothers, InuYasha and Sesshomaru, coming to blows, with their famed swords unsheathed and ready to do damage. Below them, in English, is printed InuYasha THE MOVIE Swords of an Honorable Ruler. Remarkably, there are no spelling errors.

Swirls of what look like red mist are printed around them and in the foreground, almost Soviet-like, is a crescent moon cut through with the staff of Miroku.

It is not a bad piece of merchandizing, and in the dog days of summer, you could do worse then fork out 4 bucks for one.

Movic
$4.00
Size 20 cm x 20 cm
© Takahashi Rumiko/Shogakkan/
Yomiuri TV/Sunrise 2000

InuYasha Chocolates and Cookies

Being part dog, InuYasha must loves sweets. Add that to the fact that he hangs around mostly with kids and, bingo!, any ingenious cookie maker has a market ready and salivating.

Enter TI, Tokyo's fine purveyor of sweet things. Not only has the company identified the lack of edible InuYasha goods on today's store shelves and done something about it, but it has also come up with some very interesting variations. If you get the chance, wrap your tongue around some of these.

InuYasha Chocolate Crunch: Lashings of individually wrapped crunchy chocolate snacks in an originally designed collectors can. Befitting the fact that sales are limited to the Tokyo area, the can's design depicts the InuYasha gang over a backdrop of Tokyo. $6.00 per can

InuYasha Cookies: Again in a can and limited to the Tokyo area, these creamy cookies are just the thing to start InuYasha's tail awagging, if he had one. The cutely drawn characters on the can are sure to make this a collectors dream item. $6.00 per can

Glossary
and
Keyword
Index

Glossary

A

Amakoi no Hoko (The Halberd of Amakoi)

The sacred treasure belonging to the true Water God, the halberd is stolen by the false Water God. It seems to work something like a bearer bond - if you possess it, then the goods are yours. Or, in the world of InuYasha, if you've got it, you're God!

The halberd displays absolute strength in attack, and also has the power to allow the Water God to revert to its true size. It is possibly modeled on the three sacred emblems of the Japanese imperial family.

Aooni

The demon that Sesshomaru kills in his quest for a strong replacement arm. We never actually get to see the fully-formed demon - just his torn off arm attached to the body of Sesshomaru.

Aun

The double-headed dragon that Sesshomaru rides. The name did not appear in the original manga, but was added in the anime version. The name is similar to the Japanese expression, "aun no kokyu" - meaning "to be in synch." 98

B

Benikasumi

The name of the sword used by Yura. It cuts flesh and bone, but leaves hair intact.

Black Priestess , The (Kuro Miko Tsubaki)

This evil miko sells her soul to the demons for eternal youth and beauty. She once viewed Kikyo as a rival, and to add injury to insult, apart from not being trusted with the job of cleansing the Shikon jewel, she also suffered an ugly injury to her face, for which she has never forgiv-

en Kikyo. Curses Kagome on Naraku's say-so, but Kagome is Kikyo's reincarnation and has the same powers to repel the curse. Although she loses out in the fight with Kagome too, she neither dies nor disappears. There is every chance we may see her again!
117-118, 119

Bodokumen
The mask that Sango wears heading into battle.

Bokuseno
The 200-year-old tree, who's branches were used to create the scabbards for Tessaiga and Tenseiga. Friends with both InuYasha and Sesshomaru.

Bunshin
One of Shippo's demonic techniques that uses the leaves of a tree.

Buyo
Kagome's daft cat. It is Buyo she is looking for when she falls into the well at the start of InuYasha, and goes through the time warp back to the Era of Warring States.
39-40, 41

Byakki Komori (Demon Bats)
A tribe of demons living in a cave in the west country. The tribe includes Tsukyumaru, Taigokumaru, respectively, father and grandfather of the demi-demon Shiori. The bats attack animals and humans and drink their blood.

D

Demons, et al
Normally translated as "yokai," but the original anime version of InuYasha often refers to them as "mononoke."
15-17, 18, 19, 23, 24, 25-26, 27, 29-31, 35, 47-48, 49-50, 55-56, 59-60, 63-64, 65-66, 67, 73, 74, 77-78, 79-80, 81-82, 83-84, 89-90, 93-94, 98, 101-102, 103, 105, 107-108, 109, 111-112, 113, 114, 117-118, 127, 129-130

Dokufun (Poisonous Powders)
The attack Sango uses against InuYasha when she at first views him as an enemy. She figures that anyone with ears like that must have a poor sense of smell.

E

Era of Warring States, The (Sengoku Jidai)
The historical period of civil wars and human upheaval in which InuYasha is set.
15-17, 39-40, 41, 43-45, 53-54

Exterminators (Taijiya)
The demon exterminators. Sango's village bases its livelihood on ridding the world of demons.
47-48

F

False Water God
Originally a sprite that lived in the lake, he cheats the true Water God, imprisoning her in a rock, and stealing her sacred treasure - the Amakoi Halberd. Demands that the villagers send their children as sacrifices, but falls to InuYasha and Taromaru.

Father of InuYasha
Like his mother, InuYasha's father is also dead before the story begins. He is remembered by all as a masterful demon who used the west as his base. Just for good measure, the grave of InuYasha's father is contained in a black pearl stored in InuYasha's right eye.

Both InuYasha's Tessaiga and Sesshomaru's Tenseiga were made from their father's fangs. The former was originally made to protect InuYasha's mother, and the latter to restore human life. From this we can see that InuYasha's father was not just a rampaging demon, but was also considerate to humans.

Fukitsu no Kumo (Miroku's Trickery)
This is the trick that Miroku uses to wheedle his way into homes on the pretext of exorcising demons. In fact, he is really just looking to secure a bed for the night.

Fujin no Mai (Dance of the Wind-Blades)
One of Kagura's demonic techniques.

G

Gaki (Hungry Demons)
In Buddhism, those who have com-

mitted wrongful deeds in a previous life are condemned to reappear in a cycle of perpetual hunger as Gaki, which are invisible to humans. But in InuYasha, Kikyo can see the Gaki who prey on those near death, and can save them from the demons. Tenseiga can also save a life by taking one sent from the other world.

Gatenmaru

Imprisons InuYasha and Miroku in a cocoon of silk in order to steal the Tessaiga, but only succeeds in making InuYasha revert to his demon origins. Spews poisonous powder and cocoons from its mouth when in human form. He is killed off so quickly by InuYasha that we never get to know too much about his demonic qualities.

Genkeisatsu

A demonic technique used by Naraku. When the negative powers in a victim's heart come into contact with Naraku's tentacle-like feelers, the victim is taken over by a dark or negative apparition, which eats away at the soul. It did not work on Kagome, but InuYasha, Miroku and Sango are all troubled by nightmares and are brought close to death. Shippo also had nightmares, probably involving his father.

Ginta

Appears in the manga as Koga's friend, but has to wait until the anime series to acquire a name. Hangs out with Hakkaku.

Gokurakucho (Birds of Paradise)

Sworn enemies of Koga's demon-wolf tribe. Not particularly strong, but tend to attack in flocks. The chief carries a shard of the Shikon jewel.

Goshinki

The third-born spawn of Naraku. Capable of looking into the hearts of men, but none too clever. Bit out a chunk of Tessaiga, which resulted in InuYasha morphing into a full-fledged demon that promptly killed Goshinki. Sesshomaru ordered Kaijinbo to forge the evil blade - Tokijin - using Goshinki's fang. Therefore, Goshinki now hangs from the hip of InuYasha's elder brother!
91-92, 97, 113

Granddad
Kagome's grandfather and guardian of the Higurashi Shrine, of whose historical roots he loves to rattle on about.

H

Hebi no Nukegara (Discarded Skin of a Snake)
The reward that Shippo receives for piggy-backing an old person with a sprained ankle to the village. Shippo is dead pleased!

Henge (Changes)
The changes that InuYasha goes through, just like a demon full-blood. A line appears across his face and his eyes become more demon-like. Seems that the scent of his blood also changes at these times.

Hiraikotsu (Boomerang)
Sango's weapon of choice. Powerful, but difficult to carry around.

Hive of the Saimyosho
The object Naraku gives to Sesshomaru, and which also prevents Miroku using his black hole as a weapon.

Hiyoshimaru
Nobunaga's pet monkey. Hiyoshimaru was the childhood name of Hideyoshi Toyotomi, another historical Japanese figure.

Hojo
Classmate of Kagome's. He likes her a lot, and buys her the health sandals. He is a good, bright kid, but never seems to make it to their dates. The Hojo was also a famous warrior family from Japanese history.
53-54

Honeguiido (Bone-Eating Well)
The well in the modern-day Higurashi Shrine. Was originally in the forest that InuYasha lived in the Era of Warring States. Though InuYasha and Kagome are the only two people who can pass through the well to the other side, it connects the two periods. (Having said which, Mistress Centipede and Yura also pass through it)

I

InuYasha

The demi-demon himself, InuYasha is some 15 years old in human terms when we first meet up with him. He was born of a human mother and a demon father. His dog ears, although cute, resemble the skins in which spicy Chinese dumplings are cooked.

InuYasha is sealed in the sacred tree by Kikyo's arrow, and released 50 years later by Kagome. He originally wanted to track down the Shikon jewel so he could become a demon full-blood. But after meeting Kikyo, he decides to become human and live out his days with the woman he loves.

InuYasha wields the powerfully destructive Tessaiga - a sword made from one of his father's fangs. He also uses such fighting techniques as the Sankontesso and Hijin Kesso.

According to the reputable Japanese reference work - the Kojien - Yaksha is the Japanese version of the name of a divine spirit who lived in the woods in Indian mythology. While feared as a demon-god who killed humans, Yaksha was also celebrated as the god of wealth. In Japan, Yasha also became one of the Hachibushu - the eight guardians of the Buddhist law after the Hindu gods had converted to Buddhism.

15-17, 18, 19, 21-22, 23, 24, 25-26, 27, 29-31, 33-34, 35, 39-40, 43-45, 46, 49-50, 55-56, 61, 69-70, 77-78, 79-80, 83-84, 85, 89-90, 91-92, 93-94, 95-96, 97, 101-102, 103, 105, 107-108, 109, 119, 123, 127, 129-130

InuYasha no Mori
(The Forest of InuYasha)

The forest no longer exists, and the area is now part of the Higurashi Shrine, along with the Honegui Well (Bone-eating Well). Kagome's home is where the original forest was thought to have been, and she can sense the poisonous cloud the forest once gave off.

Izayoi

Izayoi is the human mother of the demi-demon InuYasha. She has already passed away by the time the story begins, so we only get flashbacks. Based on her appearance in those flashbacks, apart from being young and beautiful, she appears to have been a woman of some social standing. Yet, her long black hair and the 12-layered

kimono she wears point to her being a Heian noblewoman, which throws the chronology of the story into some doubt.
21-22

J

Jaken
Retainer of Sesshomaru, in much the same way that Myogajii serves InuYasha. But Jaken is the real thing, a thoroughly loyal family follower suggesting a relationship based on trust.
73, 98

Jewel Fragments
The shards of the splintered Shikon jewel. Nobody knows how many there are - meaning nobody knows how long the search for all the fragments will continue.

Jinenji
A demi-demon of terrible appearance, but kind of heart. Physically strong, he works in his fields by day. The villagers believe he is a man-eating demon, and set out to kill him, but Kagome protects him, and helps to resolve the age-old prejudice of the villagers.

Jizo
A technique used by Shippo.

Juromaru (One of the Evil Twins)
Spawned by Naraku, but listens only to his evil counterpart - Kageromaru - and lops off Naraku's head the moment he is born. Slides up the blade of Tessaiga at one stage. A real slug on a razor's edge!
113

Juzu (Beads)
A long rosary of beads that Miroku winds around the hand with the black hole in it to effectively block it off.
63-64

K

Kaede
The younger sister of Kikyo and also a miko priestess. Kaede is one of the first people to realize that Kagome is the reincarnation of her beautiful elder sister, though they are not at all alike. She was still a child when InuYasha was sealed up in the sacred tree, and did not wear her

characteristic eye-pad until InuYasha seized the jewel, leading us to think she lost the eye as a result of that incident. She is still a practicing priestess 50 years after her sister's death, and becomes a dependable adviser to InuYasha and Kagome.
18, 25-26, 39-40, 125, 127, 129-130

Kagami (Kanna's Mirror)
Kanna's mirror is capable of sucking out the soul of anything reflected in its glass, and can repel an attack even from something as powerful as Tessaiga. It can also conjure up goings-on many miles from where Kanna is.

Kageromaru
The fourth-born demon of Naraku, but kept inside Juromaro like a parasite. This is some wild demon, who even chops off Naraku's head the moment he is born. He has small, folded arms like a mantis and talks a lot.
113

Kagewaki Hitomi
When Sango and the exterminators are called to rid his castle of demons, everyone ends up dead except for Sango. That's because Kagewaki is really just a convenient front for Naraku.
105, 107-108

Kagura
The second-born demon of Naraku who controls the wind. She is a 17-year-old, fan-carrying free and independent spirit, just like the wind, and openly resents the control exercised over her by Naraku. She plots against her maker, and tries to win Sesshomaru to her side. But Naraku literally has her heart in his hands, and can destroy her at will, so she is between a rock and a hard place. Her techniques include Shibu, Dance of the Wind-Blade, and Dance of the Serpent.
113

Kaijinbo
(The Cast-Out Sword Smith)
The name of the sword smith and expelled apprentice of Totosai. He is cast out of the workshop because he makes swords dripping in pure evil. He also appears to have led a wasted life.

He makes the Tokijin sword from one of Goshinki's fangs, but he himself is overwhelmed by its evil.

He attacks InuYasha, only to be cut into little pieces by the revitalized Tessaiga. A lei of skulls is his trademark.
91-92, 97

Kanna
The firstborn demon of Naraku, but second to appear after her sister Kagura. Owner of an all-powerful mirror. Said to be about 10 years old and very obedient, unlike her sister Kagura.
113

Kappa (Water Sprites)
InuYasha runs into them in his quest for the Shikon jewel and asks them a few questions. In the Japanese version of the anime, they speak with broad Osaka accents, which makes them sound like stand-up comedians. They are none too clever.

Kazana
The black hole in Miroku's hand that serves as a force field, sucking everything in. It can make light work of anything even as heavy as 700 kgs, and has a range of about 100 meters. The hole is the result of a curse put on Miroku's grandfather by Naraku, and has stayed in the family, sucking in both his grandfather and father. For Miroku it is a race against time, as he must kill Naraku and remove the curse before he himself is sucked into the void.
61, 63-64, 69-70, 71, 105, 114

Kaze no Kizu (Wind Wound)
The essential Tessaiga technique that exhibits its full power as a weapon. First proved by Sesshomaru, the technique is capable of killing 100 demons with a single stroke. Useful up to 80 meters, which makes it slightly inferior to Miroku's black hole.
29-31, 91-92

Kemukujara
The remains of demons cast off by Naraku, but reanimated by contact with the shard of the Shikon jewel carried by Koga.

Kikyo
The miko with the mostest. Good looking, and able to cleanse the demonic powers of the odd magical orb or two, Kikyo developed feelings for InuYasha while she was alive, contravening her role in serv-

ing the gods alone. However, she died hating him after being tricked by Naraku. She is brought back to life by Urasue, and after killing her now cares for the sick and the injured in the shrine. Kikyo is a multifaceted character who, because the series is ongoing, could still play a major role in the outcome of the story.
24, 25-26, 33-34, 39-40, 41, 43-45, 46, 47-48, 51, 55-56, 77-78, 79-80, 81-82, 83-84, 85, 101-102, 103, 105, 107-108, 117-118, 119, 127

Kirara

Sango's pet cat demon. A cute cat with two tails, clever, loving, and looks as though we should all have one at home. When the fight is on, however, it morphs into a fierce, flying, phalanx of fluff. In the anime version of InuYasha, Kirara - or her ancestors - fought alongside Midoriko.

Koga

At just 15 years of age in human terms, he is the young chief of the demon-wolf tribe. A rough and ready type, as befits the leader of a pack of wolves and those in human form. He possesses a shard of the Shikon jewel, and the fastest legs around. Has taken quite a shine to Kagome, and looks on InuYasha as a rival because of this. However, he is not a hateful character. Joins the InuYasha gang in order to take his revenge on Naraku for killing members of his pack.
121, 123

Kohaku

Weak-willed, cowardly 11-year-old younger brother of Sango. Was manipulated by Naraku to kill his own father, a memory he tries to erase from his mind. Was close to death himself, but is kept alive by a shard of the Shikon jewel in his body. If it is removed, he will die.
43-45

Koharu

A country-girl who Miroku met when she was 11, and in typical Miroku form, she was immediately asked to have his baby. And guess what!? She agrees! But nothing happens, as Miroku tries to make a move on Sango instead. Still, it appears the monk has some protective feelings for the girl.
43

Kokochu (Stomach Worm)

Burrows into human beings and takes control of them. Manages to enter Mushin - Miroku's teacher - and forces him to try and kill his pupil. Kokochu is raised in a jar by a jar-keeper. A ringworm-type of demon, with no powers of its own.

Kotatsu (Hell's Painter)

A painter who mixes a shard of the Shikon jewel in with human blood and liver to make his Indian ink. The images he depicts have the strange power of coming to life and doing his bidding. Although he appears to be as demonic as the next creature, Kotatsu is in fact human. He tries to paint a princess he has fallen in love with, but is devoured by the spilled ink from his inkwell.
43-45

Kotodama Beads

The string of beads placed around InuYasha's neck by Kaede. The beads react whenever Kagome calls out "Sit!" driving the demi-demon to the floor. At first he tries to remove the beads, but eventually becomes used to the strange power that helps keep the demon in him under some restraint.
25-26

Kugutsu no Jutsu (Puppet Technique)

A technique used by Naraku, where he attaches a lock of his hair to a wooden doll and creates an alter ego, which he has carry out his wishes. Naraku seldom appears in person, attempting to manipulate others to do his bidding.

Kumogashira

Demons with human heads on spiders' bodies, they have shards of the Shikon jewel lodged in them. These spiders go around in terrifying hordes attacking human beings. The chief spider was originally a Buddhist monk who looked after the young girl Nazuna, but became a totally evil demon preying on the weaknesses of human beings. He comes across InuYasha without his demon powers, but the demi-demon manages to recover and exterminate him.

Kusarigama (Chain and Sickle)

A weapon used by Kohaku - not only as one of the demon exterminators, but also after he is manipulated by Naraku. He also uses a sword.

L

Leader of the Gokurakucho
Twins who carry a shard of the jewel in their mouths. They attempt to steal Koga's jewel fragment but are dispatched by InuYasha.

M

Manten
Younger brother of Hiten and other half of the murderous Thunder Brothers. He is eventually dispatched by Tessaiga. Looks likes a cross between a giant fish and a reptile, and admires his elder brother because he has a full head of hair.

Mayu
The little girl who dies in the fire in the present day, and becomes a vengeful spirit, as she does not understand how her mother could save only her brother. Kagome explains things to her and persuades Tatari-Mokke not to guide her to hell.
15-17

Midoriko
A priestess from the ancient period when Japan was ruled by nobles. She was one of the original demon exterminators, sucking out their souls. This is how she came to acquire the Shikon jewel.
47-48

Miko (Shinto Priestess)
What Kikyo and Kaede are.
33-34, 39-40, 46, 47-48, 49-50, 51, 53-54, 65-66, 77-78, 81-82, 101-102, 119, 125

Miroku
The monk with the one-track mind, and a black hole in his hand to boot. He is deadly afraid that the curse of Naraku will hold true, and that he too will be sucked into the vortex in his hand just as his father and grandfather were. This is why he joins the quest to gather together the shards of the Shikon jewel and overthrow the Evil One. As a Buddhist monk, he is something of an anomaly. Miroku has his share of fights, frauds and female fans. His classic pick-up line is, "How's about having my baby?" The story is that before he joins the InuYasha gang, he has a success rate of around

90%! It all stops dead when he runs into Sango. Just to make him more interesting, he rides around in the Era of Warring States on a bicycle. 15-17, 46, 51, 59-60, 61, 63-64, 65-66, 67, 69-70, 71, 73, 74, 105, 114, 123, 127

Mizukami (Water God)
The true Water God is a beautiful goddess, but she is tricked by a sprite that lives in the lake, and is imprisoned in a rock.

Mizukirinoho
A technique used by the Water God.

Mo Mo
The three-eyed bull that Totosai rides, but has also been known to carry InuYasha and Myogajii. Looks a little comical with his extra eye, but is as sturdy as they come. Just so you know, "mo mo" is the sound Japanese children make to indicate a cow - "moo moo!"

Mukadejoro (Mistress Centipede)
The centipede demon that sucked the jewel from the side of Kagome. Seems that the "Joro" part of the name refers to a noblewoman, but this centipede demon is far from ladylike. She should be remembered as the one who takes Kagome back to the Era of Warring States, and for a short while at least harbors the jewel in her body. InuYasha quickly finishes her off. The change she goes through when she swallows the jewel is quite something.
41, 51

Mummified Hand of the Kappa
A birthday present for Kagome from her grandfather. The thing is much maligned by her cat Buyo, but is said to bring happiness.

Mummy
Midoriko's mummified remains are found in a cave in the demon-exterminator's village. It is a bit difficult to understand how a mummy could be kept for all those years in the particularly humid Japanese climate.

Muonna (Nothing Woman)
The combined spirits of mothers who have lost their children in battles. Thanks to one of Sesshomaru's plots, she takes the form of InuYasha's deceased mother and attempts to suck him in. But she is a

mother to the end, and eventually dies protecting InuYasha from Sesshomaru.

Musashi no Tonosama
The name of the young lord that is possessed by the demon - Tsuku no Gama. His consort - Princess Tsuyu - says the young lord is quite handsome, but there is something not quite right about these two. He gets swallowed up by the ugly toad, and she can't tell the difference.

Mushin
The monk who brought up Miroku after his father had been sucked into the vortex of the black hole. He is the only one who can tend to the hole, and Miroku trusts him entirely. In a standard family situation you would probably say - like father, like son. But apart from the fact that neither his grandfather nor father were there for Miroku, it is the boozing Mushin who sets him on his ways as a rakish man of the cloth.
71

Muso
Spawn of Naraku, literally created from throw-away parts. Has the spi-der of Onigumo on his back, kills everything that crosses his path, and is faceless until he meets and kills the monk Muso. He takes his face and his name.

Demon or cyborg? InuYasha kills Muso, but his body rapidly reforms itself, and it is clear he is not going to die until he can figure out who he is. He has no memory of his own, and keeps following the tracks of Onigumo. Naraku has tried to banish the memory of the human that keeps him from being a full-demon, but cannot pull it off. And despite discarding Muso once, he is forced to reabsorb him.

Myogajii (Flea Demon)
A long-standing retainer in the family of InuYasha. A flea just seven millimeters in size, but grows as tall as two meters after sucking up human blood. Knowledgeable but cowardly, disappearing at the first sound of a fight.
35, 129-130

N

Nanushi

The lord who tries to substitute one of the village children for his own child as a human sacrifice to the false Water God. His son tries to save his friend, and the lord is later blackmailed by Miroku for his actions.

Naraku
(The Evil One/Buddhist Hell)

The demi-demon born of Onigumo, and the common enemy of InuYasha, Miroku, Sango, Kikyo and Koga. It is fitting that one so evil should take his name from Buddhist hell. He tries everything in his power to overcome InuYasha and obtain the fragments of the Shikon jewel so he can become a demon full-blood and shake of the influence of the human Onigumo. He merges himself with other demons to increase his powers, and spawns horrific creatures to do his dirty work.

33-34, 43-45, 51, 61, 63-64, 67, 69-70, 73, 77-78, 79-80, 85, 101-102, 103, 105, 106, 107-108, 109, 111-112, 113, 114, 123

Nazuna

The name of the young girl whose father is killed by spider-head demons, and then looked after by a monk. The monk is really a spider-head too, though Nazuna, innocent as ever, does not want to believe it.

Night of the New Moon

The time of the month that the demi-demon, InuYasha, loses whatever demonic qualities he has and becomes a defenseless human being.

Nikuzukinomen
(Flesh-Eating Mask)

Carved from an ancient tree embedded with a shard of the Shikon jewel, it survives by eating people. Can sense the presence of other fragments of the jewel, which is how it comes to attack Kagome. Kagome is saved by InuYasha, who somehow manages to make it all the way from the Era of Warring States.

43-45

Ninmenka (Head-Fruit)

The live heads that the Peach Man uses as his elixir of life.

Nintojo (The Staff of Heads)
The staff carried by Jaken. It is the key to finding where InuYasha's father is buried. Can also breath fire. 98

Nobunaga (manga) - Amari (anime)
Childhood friend of Princess Tsuyu, he also harbors romantic feelings for her. Not Nobunaga Oda, but Nobunaga Takeda. Together with his monkey Hiyoshimaru, he follows her all the way to the toad's lair to save her. He has a kind heart, but not much of a brain.

O

Ogumo (Giant spider)
The spider that Sango and the group of exterminators get rid of at the behest of Naraku. The spider has no worthwhile demonic powers to speak of, and is soon vanquished.

Okamakiri (The Praying Mantis)
Okamakiri is the praying mantis that, under the orders of Naraku, changes into a beautiful princess and seduces Miroku. The monk, of course, is easily tricked, and gets

the hole in his hand opened even wider when the praying mantis is sucked in. The creature supposedly has a sister, who meets up with Miroku at Mushin's place.

Okashira (The Chief)
Head of the bandit clan and known for being not quite there. By the time he appears in the manga, he has already been killed by Shibugarasu, although few of his people seem to realize this.

Omukade
The demon that Sango extermi-nates the first time she appears. The centipede carried a shard of the Shikon jewel, which was kept at the exterminator's village until stolen by Naraku's cohort and passed on to His Evilness.

Onibikushi (Demon Comb)
One of the techniques used by Sakasagami no Yura. The comb is said to burn right through to the bone marrow. She tries it against Kagome, who is saved by InuYasha and his Hinezumi no Koromo.

Onigumo
The name of the bandit cared for by

Kikyo some 50 years before, after being badly burnt and unable to move. He then sells his body to the demons so that he may keep his rotten soul and seize the priestess who has helped him. This is how the demi-demon Naraku comes to be formed.

Because he is covered in bandages, we do not get to see his face. Along with the fact that he has combined with so many demons to become Naraku only goes to increase the feeling that he is a mystery we know very little about. 101-102, 103, 106, 107-108

Onna Yokai (Female Demon)

A female demon that Hiten turns up with. When we first see her, it is also the first time for her to meet Manten, so there is a strong chance that Hiten picked her up somewhere along the way. She is a demon wrapped in a serpent, and is killed for no apparent fault of her own by Hiten in a fit of anger. In the final analysis, she is little more than a sad, inadequate character used merely to show the depths of Hiten's cruelty.

P

Pool at the Base of the Waterfall at Forbidden Mountain

The place Kikyo goes to rest after being poisoned by Naraku. Kikyo's Shikigami has brought some of the earth from her grave, which is purified after being touched by Kagome. This earth is then poured into the wound in Kikyo's breast, cleansing it of the poison.

R

Raigekijin

Hiten's sword, which gives off thunder. Can be reined in using Tessaiga's sheath.

Rin

The little girl who sees her family killed by bandits in front of her very eyes, the shock of which steals away her power of speech. She is killed by one of Koga's pack, but brought back to life by Sesshomaru's Tenseiga. Following this, she lives to serve Sesshomaru, and goes with him everywhere. She makes a good combination with

Jaken.
95-96

Royakan
The wolf-demon. He walks around proclaiming himself, "Oyakan," the Wolf from Hell. But he is not in the least bit strong, and looks as though he just walked off the pages of a manga. He has no great ambitions of his own and possibly for that reason is easily manipulated by Naraku, who makes him attack InuYasha It is one of those rare cases where InuYasha does not kill his opponent, and after Kagome takes away his shard of the Shikon jewel, he walks off into the sunset.

Ryuja no Mai
One of Kagura's demonic techniques, by which she whips up a type of whirlwind, known as the Dragon Wind.

Ryukotsusei
The dragon-like demon that InuYasha's father fought and entombed. His coat is stronger than steel and not even InuYasha's father could finish him off. Fighting the dragon is a rite of passage for InuYasha, who must recover the power to wield Tessaiga, and surpass the exploits of his father.

    The rite of passage is achieved, and InuYasha surpasses his father when he totally masters Kaze no Kizu, uses the Bakuryuha, does not lose total control even when transformed into a demon, and manages to use the adapted Tessaiga.
19, 29-31

S

Sacred Tree
The tree in the grounds of the modern-day Higurashi Shrine, and the one in which InuYasha was sealed up for 50 years. It was already quite a tree in the warring states period.
33-34

Saimyosho (Demon Wasps)
Poisonous insects from hell that turn up everywhere Naraku goes. The Evil One uses them in an attempt to prevent Miroku using his black hole as a weapon - because if he sucked in these evil little creatures, he would soon be dead.

    They also serve as transporters and spies for Naraku. I guess

we can say they do all the dirty work that Naraku avoids while looking to stay out of the way of InuYasha or anyone who can give them a good beating.
63-64, 114

Sakasagami no Yura (Demon Hair)

Yura's sex appeal is underscored by the amount of flesh she has on display. But even though she may appear to be kawaii to the 'nth degree, she is a cruel little demon. She can control her hair at will, and uses it to search for the shards of the Shikon jewel. She is eventually killed by InuYasha and Kagome.
23

Sango

Some 16 years old when we first see her, she uses her boomerang - Hiraikotsu - to exterminate demons. Sango was born and brought up in the village of the demon exterminators, and has developed a reputation for being one of the best there is.

But the village falls prey to Naraku's plotting, and her own younger brother is manipulated to kill her father. She falls in with InuYasha in order to reap her revenge on Naraku, but when she is not out exterminating demons she is just an ordinary kid.
15-17, 43-45, 46, 47-48, 51, 69-70, 123

Sango's Father

Village headman, but killed by his own son - Kohaku - who has become caught up in Naraku's intrigues.
77-78, 117-118

Sankontesso (Claws of Steel)

One of InuYasha's fighting techniques, by which he literally tears his opponents apart with his claws. Pretty cruel for such a nice guy.
23

Sayo

The name of the little girl who lovingly looks after Kikyo in the village she goes to following her revitalization. Kikyo returns this kindness.

Scrolls

Kaede and Miroku use scrolls to restrain InuYasha when he is injured. They are also what Miroku infuses with his power before slinging them at demons.

Seikai
A virtuous monk who sees through the fact that Kikyo is no longer of this world. But his virtuous nature almost gets him killed.

Senaka no Kumo (Spider Mark)
Naraku's trademark. It appears on all his spawn like a birthmark. It is the link back to Onigumo - the source of the evil that created Naraku.

Sesshomaru
Half-brother to InuYasha and a demon full-blood. He has two distinctive lines running across his face and can actually be said to be good looking, but morphs into a terrible demon like his father when angry. Sesshomaru appears to be on a different level than the other characters in InuYasha in that he shows no interest in the Shikon jewel. The truth of the matter is he believes himself strong enough to handle most situations. But he dearly wants to get his hands on Tessaiga, so clashes with InuYasha and loses his right arm.
24, 27, 29-31, 73, 89-90, 91-92, 93-94, 95-96, 97, 98

Shakujo
The staff carried by Miroku, it has been in his family since his grandfather's time. This kind of staff, with six rings jangling around the top, is referred to as a Boddhisatva staff. It is normally carried by a monk, or some one indulging in the ascetic training of a monk, and made with a tin covering and several metal rings at the hilt. Miroku uses his staff as a weapon.

Sheath of Tessaiga
Carved out of the bark of the 200-year-old Bokuseno tree.

**Shibugarasu
(Corpse Dancing Crow)**
Three-eyed crow that feeds on human beings. Swallows the Shikon jewel early on in the story, only to be shot out of the sky by a hama no ya arrow shot by Kagome. It is because of this that Inuyasha and his gang set off on the trip to recover the shards of the jewel.
43-45

**Shikabanemai
(Dance of the Corpses)**
Demonry used by Kagura, who manipulates the dead and makes

them attack her enemies.

Shikigami
A servant of the Black Priestess, following her every word. In many ways, it is like a pet.
119

Shikon (Four Souls)
The four souls that reside in the Shikon jewel are Aramitama - the guardian of courage; Kushimitama - the guardian of knowledge; Sachimitama - the guardian of love; and Nigimitama - the guardian of affinity. These combine to become a single entity, forming the soul of a human being. According to Shinto religion, all living things are made up of four souls.

Shikon jewel
(Shikon no Tama)
The absolute entity at the center of this entire story. The jewel that grants all wishes, and has every man, dog-demon, spirit and apparition chasing after it - with the exception of Sesshomaru. The jewel is active on a 500-year cycle, sinking with Kikyo during the Era of Warring States only to reappear embedded in the left side of

Kagome in modern times.

Shinidamachu (Soul Collector)
The insect that collects dead souls to help the reanimated Kikyo keep body and soul together. Very obedient.

Shiori
A demi-demon born of a Tsukuyomaru - a bat-demon - and a human mother. Shiori has the power to set up and control force fields, and is called Protector of the Force Field by her grandfather, Taibokumaru. Shiori loves her father, and feels special pride in surpassing him in creating force fields. She also develops a unique relationship with one of the other major demi-demons in the series - InuYasha.

Shippo (Seven Treasures)
A young fox-demon. Shippo may be the only full-fledged demon in the InuYasha gang. He is on a quest for the shards of the splintered Shikon

jewel to avenge the death of his father, and throws in his lot with InuYasha.

It is near impossible to figure out how old demons are meant to be, but in human terms Shippo is around seven years of age. He is the ultimate in common sense, speaking the language of an older and maturer type. Given his age, this characteristic sometimes makes him a funny kind of creature.

He gets his friends out of tight spots on numerous occasions, playing the role of big brother to the older characters around him. He treats everyone just the same and, mentally speaking, is probably more mature than InuYasha.
43-45

Shippo's Father

A fox-demon killed by Manten because he possessed some of the shards of the Shikon jewel. He ends up being used as a loin cloth, which is somewhat disrespectful to the dead. Still, Shippo's father manages to protect Shippo and Kagome with his foxy will o' the wisp qualities. Such skills mean he must have been quite a powerful demon in his time, and suggests there are great things in store for Shippo.

Shoki (Poison)

Evil and poisonous miasma mainly exuded by demons. Naraku's very body is composed of a miasmic poison.

Sit! (Osuwari)

The words Kagome uses on InuYasha to take control of the situation. There is no way InuYasha can oppose this command, and he is thrust to the ground from the neck, or, more accurately, from the beads around his neck.
25-26

T

Taijiya no Sato (Exterminatorville)

Where Sango, her father, and her younger brother, Kohaku, all hail from. Although a fact soon forgotten, it is also the place where the Shikon jewel originated. Naraku sends in a demon army and wipes out the entire village.

Tama Hakkenki

What InuYasha says when Miroku

figures out that the demi-demon is in love with Kagome.

Tamashizume no Fue (The Magic Whistle)
The whistle that Tatari-Mokke carries.

Tamashizume no Kotodama (The Magical Words)
Specifically refers to Kagome telling InuYasha "Sit!"

Taromaru
The high-born child designated to be the live sacrifice for the false Water God, but switched for the village child - Suekichi - Taromaru's friend. Taromaru joins with InuYasha to fight the false Water God and save his friend.

Tatari-Mokke
A benevolent demon, whose job is to watch over the souls of children until they become Buddhas. Tries to take the sad child Mayu to hell, but is persuaded not to do so by Kagome.

Tenseiga (Life-Giving Blade)
Sesshomaru's blade - also made from the fangs of InuYasha's father.

A caring, curing sword.
19, 93-94, 95-96

Tessaiga (Steel Pulverizer)
InuYasha's blade, and one of the swords made from the fangs of InuYasha's father. Cannot be wielded by full-blooded demons such as Sesshomaru. Has the effect of reining in InuYasha's demon instincts.
23, 25-26, 27, 29-31, 63-64, 67, 89-90, 91-92, 93-94, 97, 129-130

Tokajin (Peach Man)
Originally human, but has assumed the position of the wise old hermit, by killing him and eating him. Has somehow come by one of the shards of the Shikon jewel, which makes it easy for him to repel InuYasha and Tessaiga. Tokajin shrinks InuYasha and swallows him whole. A combination of Kagome's charmed arrow and InuYasha's full-frontal attack forces him off the top of a cliff and eventually kills him.

Tokijin (Demon Sword)
The demon sword made from one of the fangs of Goshinki that chewed right through Tessaiga. Forged by Kaijinbo on the orders of Sesshomaru, it's a bad-news evil

blade. It drives Kaijinbo himself totally mad, and he chases after InuYasha only to be killed by a reconstituted Tessaiga.
91-92, 97

Totosai (Sword Smith)
The original funky forger of do-good steel. Forged both Tessaiga and Tenseiga. Only works for those he likes - but doesn't really like Sesshomaru. Also repairs Sango's boomerang - Hiraikotsu. Wanders around with a three-eyed bull.
29-31, 93-94, 97, 129-130

Tsubotsukai (Jar-Keeper)
A demon who breeds insects that burrow into people and control them. It is the insects that are the killers - the keeper is a weakling.

Tsubushigoma
A demon-fox technique used by Shippo. Looks like the real McCoy, but when it comes down to it, is just smoke and mirrors.

Tsukumo no Gama (Demon Toad)
The toad who takes over the body of the lord of the manor, Princess Tsuyu's husband, and eats the souls of the local virgins. Not strong, but

tricky, and it takes some quick thinking by Kagome to exterminate him good and proper.

Tsuyuhime (Princess Tsuyu)
She may be beautiful, but the princess isn't the brightest kid on the block. Especially as she can't even figure out that the toad is not the man she is betrothed to.

U

Urasue
Urasue is the demon who brings Kikyo back from the dead using bones and the earth from her grave. She tries to have the reanimated Kikyo search out the shards of the Shikon jewel for her, but is killed instead, leaving not much room for character development. Let's just say her biggest error was bringing Kikyo back to life.
33-34, 55-56, 81-82, 127

W

Wolf-Demons
Koga's tribe. Some are full-fledged wolves, and some are in human

form, they live in the cave behind the waterfall. Koga is gifted with a shard of the Shikon jewel, which makes him ultra fast. In many scenes we see him panting after the chase. Cruel as only wolves can be, given the lives they lead, on an individual basis there are some decent guys among the tribe. Once Koga takes a shine to Kagome and calls her his woman, the rest of the tribe accept her as one of their own, referring to her as "ne-san," or "big sister."

121

Y

Yumi (The Way of the Bow)
Kikyo is an expert with the bow. It follows that Kagome has also acquired some of these skills too. It is from Kagome's bow that the charmed arrow is let loose, setting the story of InuYasha on its way. Still, Kagome has much to learn - it is a missed shot that sends Manten into fit of rage.

Keyword Index

T

U

Y

From character goods to on-screen anime stars, the MYSTERIES AND SECRETS REVEALED! series brings you everything you never knew and more about your favorite anime and manga characters. Compiled in Tokyo, Japan, home of otaku culture, this series is unofficial and unrelenting in its quest to unearth the mysteries and secrets behind some of the world's most popular anime!

Coming soon in the MYSTERIES AND SECRETS REVEALED! series

YuYu Hakusho
The Complete Guide

Since its manga launch in 1990, which sold 40 million copies in Japan, to the hit series on Cartoon Network, YuYu Hakusho has attracted anime fans of all stripes. The adventures of Yusuke, a tough teen delinquent who dies saving a child from a traffic accident and is reborn as a Spirit Detective, are played out in a fast-paced multi-dimensional world of supernatural baddies and doting teenage girls. **YuYu Hakusho: The Complete Guide** takes the reader on a whirlwind tour through Yusuke's many worlds, unearthing and explaining everything from story backgrounds and characters quirks to supernatural technologies and merchandise hot on the streets of Tokyo.

$11.95   ISBN 1-932897-09-7   October 2004

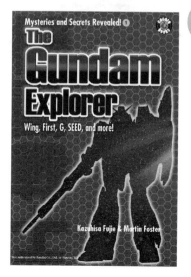

MYSTERIES AND SECRETS REVEALED! 1
The
Gundam Explorer
Wing, First, G, SEED, and more!

Why does Char wear a mask?
Who or what is Shubertz Bruder?
What is Operation Meteor?
How does OMNI differ from the UESA?

Mobile Suit Gundam is recognized as the masterpiece of robot anime. The first TV show, which began in Japan in 1979, launched a series of feature animation that today still manages to wow even the most jaded mecha fan.

The Gundam Explorer reveals the mysteries and secrets of four televised Gundam sagas. From Wind, First and G to the newly-released SEED, this book guides the reader through a maze of character bios, Gundam technologies and truths and legends that continue to perplex and mesmerize fans all over the world.

$11.95   ISBN 0-9723124-8-X

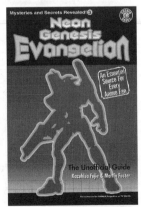